be ye

by Mary Banks

Copyright © 2006

Mary Banks Ministries, Inc.

info@marybanks.net

Table of Contents

About the Author
MARY BANKS

Mary Banks is an apostle and founder of many churches under the banner of Bible Teachers International, a division of Mary Banks Ministries, Inc. Bible Teachers International Worship Centers and Mary Banks Global Training Centers are now located throughout the United States, Canada, the Caribbean Islands, India and London with new doors of opportunity opening everyday. She is "The Bible Teacher," an international speaker, minister of the gospel and author of many books and courses that have brought a sure word to the Body of Christ.

Mary Banks is also the founder and president of **Lifesavers International,** a Christian Evangelistic Recovery Program that reaches out to the lost at their point of need. She has been instrumental in the salvation, recovery and development of many who had previously been bound by drugs, damaged emotions and other powerful captivities! Many who have been set free through her Recovery Programs are now operating Lifesavers Clinics, Online Internet Counseling Forums and Bible classes internationally.

Mary Banks has touched the hearts and souls of thousands held captive by crack cocaine, depression, alcoholism and "lives without purpose" through: her crusades, street ministries, schools of ministries, Schools of the Prophets, dramatic productions with Bible Theater, books and instructional audio and video media, as well as her Mary Banks Global Training Center Website (www.bibleteachers.com) which offers a "virtual classroom" with online video courses available 24 hours a day worldwide.

She received the **Martin Luther King Award in 1996**, which was presented to her by Governor Lawton Chiles of Florida in recognition of her contributions and teachings throughout the State of Florida. In addition, she received a Proclamation from the Dade County Board of Commissioners in Miami for her spiritual and cultural contributions to society, as well as her giftedness as a Christian playwright in her production of "The Potter's House." December 29th has been heralded as "The Potter's House Day" in Dade County, Florida by Commissioner James C. Burke. (See the newest gospel productions and details at the **Bible Theater International website www.bibletheater.com**)

In 1998, The National Association of Negro Business and Professional Women's Club, Inc. selected Dr. Banks to be honored as one of the outstanding female pastors of Broward County for her significant contribution to the spiritual growth of the South Florida community.

The apostle is careful to make it known that the degree or title of Dr. Banks is honorary in nature and was bestowed upon her by an institution recognizing her years of ministry, as well as ministerial curriculum development for the education and training of ministers, and the development and installation of spiritually-based clinical recovery programs that have brought deliverance to souls worldwide. Thus it is her desire to make it known that the revelations that have brought many, who attend her churches and ministerial training schools throughout America and abroad to that place of spiritual perfection did not come as a result of her being formally educated, but by a face to face visitation from our Lord and Savior Jesus Christ.

Foreword

Congratulations. You have dared to open a book with a title as audacious as "Be Ye Perfect." Perhaps you were drawn to these words out of morbid curiosity, or better yet, ardent skepticism. For who could possibly be perfect except God and what difference would it make anyway?

But perhaps, like we first were and like Mary Banks certainly was, you were drawn to these words, to the idea of perfection, out of pure and simple desperation. Desperation nurtured through years of fruitless struggle, contention, and warfare both within yourself and with the powers around you to be holy, to be righteous, to be anything but who you knew yourself to be; a desperation that left you balancing on the razor's edge of realization that either there had to be more to Christianity than what has been taught or Christianity itself is just as disposable as every other philosophy or religion out there today.

The book you hold in your hands is no fad teaching, no new trendy religious thinking. The truths and revelation found here won't be finding their way to charm bracelets, inspirational candy wrappers or witty T-shirts. No, the truths Mary Banks so engagingly present represent nothing short of a revolution. The church must either embrace it or they will be the ones who are truly left behind.

The reason we can so boldly proclaim this is that though we have known Mary only a short time, the revelation that God has walked her through and that you will discover in this book was, unbeknownst to us, the very same revelation He has spent the last six years cultivating in our own lives. It was a revelation that brought us to our knees, caused us to become, for the first time, truly "born again," and even led to the writing of our own book on the subject entitled "The Secret Place." We had set out to create a simple document that would serve as something akin to a mission statement for Gener8Xion Entertainment. The result was not a mission statement for our company. It was a mission statement for our lives. And while we didn't do much more than give our book away to friends and family, it seems God is now ready to take this word to the nations.

How many times over the years did we ourselves wonder about the lack of change, the lack of power in our own lives to be who we thought Christ was calling us to be? But then again, everyone seemed to be in the same predicament. How was it that being "born-again" left us all with the same pain, struggles and weaknesses as the next guy? Was the only thing different about a Christian in whom the Kingdom of God supposedly dwelt that they simply got out of Hell when they died? When we proclaimed, "I have been crucified with Christ, but it is no longer I who live but Christ lives in me," did it really mean that there was no difference between us and someone who hadn't been crucified with Christ? Or was Christ's blood such that *sometimes* we had the ability to be more Christ-like, but that the power tended to ebb and flow, like energy boosts in a video game…sometimes it was there, giving us an inkling of divine power, but the rest of the time we were cursed with being "only human?"

How refreshing it is to see that these were the very same questions plaguing Mary on her journey. She writes: *"When the rubber met the road, we were still crippled by emotional pains, suppressing true desires and struggling to maintain righteous character on a daily basis. We went to conventions and conferences looking for the magic formula. We wanted to hear something that would end the struggle and cause us to walk in the power of the Holy Ghost. We knew enough to know that we were missing something, but because we didn't know what it was that we lacked, we continued to hunger and search for the knowledge, the prophecy or the laying on of hands that would finally catapult us into that long sought after place of power."*

How many more laying on of hands *is* it going take, how many revival meetings? How many books for that matter? How many books, that is, unlike this one, that philosophize and twist scripture toward man's intentions rather than God's?

The main thesis of this book can be summed up with Mary's statement on page 14: *"...you must accept the fact that **the true meaning of sonship is a perfect, sinless identity.** If not, you will never expect to live a life that is pleasing to the Father. You will always vacillate back and forth in and out of righteousness."*

A sinless identity. How interesting that this is the very essence, the very reality that God first shared with us through a humble pastor named Gary Zamora who, as God would have it, used the very same words to describe our intended relationship with Christ.

What's more, Mary writes that God gave her this revelation some twenty something years ago, but told her that she could not write about it until she built a congregation that was the living proof of the power of this word. In the same way, the Lord kept our pastor and his wife hidden on the "back-side of the desert" in Tucson, Arizona, for twenty-two years awaiting a season in which they could step forth with the very same word that would bring freedom to the church and lead this generation into the Promised Land of our inheritance through Christ.

Words simply cannot express how amazing and awe-inspiring it is to be given a glimpse into how God is moving in these exciting days we now live. We knew that when God, by His grace, shared with us His heart and the revelation of our true identity in Christ, it would be the catalyst to literally change the nations of the earth; but like Elijah, we had no idea just how many others He had hidden away for such a time as this.

Many of us have waited a long time for that little cloud of possibility to come in from over the ocean, bringing with it the much needed rain of transformation. With confidence, we can now proclaim that the rain has come. So drink it in, for His yoke is easy and His burden is light. Go, be ye perfect and fulfill your destiny!

March 29, 2006

Matthew & Laurie Crouch
Chairman/CEO,
Gener8Xion Entertainment

Stephan & Jennifer Blinn –
VP Production & Development
Gener8Xion Entertainment

Richard & Maria Cook
VP/General Manager,
Gener8Xion Entertainment

A Prophetic Word

It is almost an understatement to say that God has an intensely passionate desire for His body, the Church, to manifest the perfection that He calls for when He says: "Be ye perfect, even as your Father which is in heaven is perfect." Together with His passion is His awesome, holy, sovereign design to satisfy His heart's desire. Experiences in my own life testify to this design, as you will see from the brief episodes, which follow.

Many years before God's sovereignty connected me with Mary Banks Ministries, in the early 90s, He prophetically spoke to me two powerful, but greatly disturbing words. The first prophecy was this: "You (meaning His people) are holding on to 'truth' just as if you are holding on to the column of a building that is not firmly cemented into a foundation." "Teach me Your truth, Father", was my response to Him, as I would lay out, face down pleading with Him.

The next prophecy was closely related, and also very direct. God said this: "You (again meaning His people) do not have My concept of My Church, but I am going to teach you My concept". Then He gave a directive: "When I have given you My vision of My Church, hold it high, and run with it."

By these two prophecies God had lodged in my breast something far more precious than gold, which I clutched and would not let go. Was He faithful in revealing His heart concerning these two critical prophecies? Yes, He was, and profoundly so. This is the story, captured in very few words.

God's sovereignty executed a Jamaica-U.S.A. connection by depositing me into Mary Banks Ministries. Through the dynamic, meticulous, Word-driven, and liberating teaching of Dr. Banks on holiness and faith, God was answering my heart's cry for His revelation on 'Truth' and 'Church'.

As you read this book, *"Be Ye Perfect"*, you will discover that the author effectively reveals the heart of God concerning His desire for His people to be perfect. Her method is to rely heavily on the Scriptures, the Word of Truth, which she allows to speak for themselves. She adopts the approach of using the Word to confirm the Word. It is my great delight that the Father has faithfully connected the prophecies about His Truth, and His Church, which He gave to me such a long time ago, with the production of this book which focuses on God's truth about His Church.

"Be Ye Perfect" demonstrates Dr. Banks' God-given love for the Church of Jesus Christ, and her zeal to see the Church transformed here and now into the glorious body that God has ordained for us to be.

You hold in your hand an excellent, comprehensive book, expressing the heart of the gospel of Jesus Christ. It is the deep calling us into the deep. I see this book as an end-time instrument to motivate God's people to give ourselves over, with the greatest urgency, to manifest the perfect image of Jesus. My prayer, as I write, is that the Holy Spirit will use the contents and the spirit of this book to instruct His people across the earth, transforming us into the Perfect Bride that Jesus is coming soon to take unto Himself.

Hazel M. Salmon
Prophetess

HOPE DEFERRED…

Before I came into the revelation of perfection through the life of Christ within me, I believed, even as most Christians, that the fleshy mind was my worst enemy; but then I read that it is with the mind that I serve the Lord, *(Romans 7:25).* So then, if the mind is the mechanism by which I am to serve the Lord, why was it always the culprit in my failures? I am sure most of you have felt the same frustrations and sense of hopelessness.

The following is an exert from my book, "The Thought War." *I wanted to live a life that was pleasing to God and also wanted to walk in the power realm of the Spirit. I had great hopes of spiritual accomplishments in ministry; I was to be like Paul, Peter and John. I would be one whose very shadow would heal the sick. What I became however was a born again believer constantly missing the mark, crippled by my emotions and depressed by life. I learned how to suppress the hurt of offenses and to hide my insecurities and low self-worth. I was married with children, but felt sad and lonely all the time. My new life as a Christian had not changed any of these "personal" issues. I knew I had received the Holy Spirit, but after the first few weeks the "new convert" excitement faded into the unexpected reality of the trials of my faith.*

Though I was loyal to all my church services and activities, the word I had received trained me to fail in God. It made me expect to miss the mark periodically. Oh, it was a stickler against fornication, adultery, drinking and other vices, but it never arrested the evil thoughts, negative character or *painful emotions I suffered year after year. Its basic theme was, "Nobody is perfect", thus it created a belief system that accepted occasional sin as a way of life. As I heard my daughter, Tanya say, **"There was no way this sinless Christ could relate to me in any place other than atonement."** His life and mine were totally separate in character and desire.*

Furthermore, the prosperity message re-created in me a thirst for worldly success. I wanted the things of this world; money, notoriety, and the good life, but Christ said to take no thought for such. I suppressed hurts and deep emotional pain in the name of bearing the infirmities of others. The apostle Paul insisted that the Corinthians walk in perfection, (2 Corinthians 13:11 Finally, brethren, farewell. Be perfect, be of good comfort, be of one mind, live in peace; and the God of love and peace shall be with you. KJV). However, the message to my church declared perfection to be <u>unobtainable</u> for the saints of God. This drove me to a place where my mind collapsed under the weight of wantonness, frustration, fear, pain and confusion.

I was a good saint, I lived as holy as I knew how or was expected to, and I definitely believed what I was taught to be the promises of God for the church. Even so, as a loyal, tithe-paying, always-there, faithful Christian, preacher and head of our women's missionary department, my mind slipped into the darkness of depression. For months I could not function in the very things that I had once been so proficient in. I neglected my business and allowed it to slowly deteriorate into nothing. I could focus on nothing; therefore working was next to impossible. I had nothing and did nothing. But to top it all off, I allowed my three children to go live with their father, who at the time was anything but a Christian. I pulled all the curtains in my three-bedroom, two-bath home, locked all the doors, turned off the lights and there I sat in the darkness until I lost sight of days, even weeks.

As I sat on the floor peering into the darkness, a movie projector was turned on in my head. It played the same feature day and night. It began with a nine-month old baby given away by her father to his hardworking, fifty-something year old, ex-wife. Though provided for, the child grew up on migrant labor camps never hearing the word "love" in the house or without. There were no hugs or parental kisses, no helping with homework nor interests in the goings on of the day, just food and shelter.

Then there was that marriage; a union between two people who had absolutely nothing in common. He was supposed to be the eighteen-year-olds' ticket out of poverty and that middle-of-nowhere farm town that had become her dead-end street; but the lack of ambition and infidelity shattered all her dreams. Oh what longing and emptiness she felt, as well as the despair of failure and betrayal.

Then came a great light! God came into her life bringing a new hope of change and fulfillment. Maybe now the marriage would truly be a marriage, and if she prayed and sought the Lord in earnest, her husband would get saved and give her the love she had never experienced. But he left, and there was nothing left for her but hard work and three children to care for.

She wonders: "Where are the promises of God? Where is the peace and prosperity she and others preached about? Where is God? Has He abandoned her too? Isn't He supposed to be her Father?" But she knows that God is holy and righteous and pure. He is love. Even so, why can't she feel His love? Why doesn't He appear out of the darkness? The answer is simple. He doesn't appear because He is not there. She is alone. The picture fades to black and there is nothing until the projector rewinds itself and the feature starts all over again.

I don't remember how or why I finally came out of that house. What I do remember is struggling to push my way back to the faith I had in a God I could not hear from. Through all of this I was able to persevere in going back to the church and maintaining my church duties. Disillusioned and disappointed I drifted through our denominational formalities and events. But somehow I knew enough to know that this was not what the Father intended to be the life of a Son.

Nevertheless, over the years I continued to fall and get up so many times until I nearly came to believe the songwriter who said, *"a saint is just a sinner who falls down and gets back up."* But thank God for His faithfulness! He allowed me to discover that the knowledge of Christ is the power to stand. ***"I didn't know what it was that I didn't know."***

In other words, I was ignorant of things pertaining to my salvation that the traditional church was just as ignorant of. I found that in the first twelve years of my new life as a born again Christian, I had not been taught the very basics of salvation. I knew nothing of the riches of God's glory that had been given to me so freely and were able to keep me from ever falling or failing God. No one told me I could be perfect in my walk of faith, in fact, I was told just the opposite. I never knew that the righteousness, peace and joy in the Holy Ghost was more than a message, or that it was my dwelling place in Christ. The word that was supposed to renew my mind and enable me to stand against the wiles of the devil was corrupted thus aiding and abetting my spiritual demise.

How was it possible to successfully work the ministry in the lives of others when so much was wrong with me? I couldn't produce anything greater than what I, myself had become. I was at the end of my faith and myself. It was then that the Lord in His tender mercy and loving-kindness stepped in to rescue me. He knew my heart really did pant after Him and that I was at a place of complete brokenness and willing indeed to listen and obey His voice.

Chapter One
THE VISITATION

It was a perfect day for studying the Word; the children were in school, the house was quiet and a glitter of sunlight danced on the blue water in the swimming pool. I was sitting in my living room on the sofa reading my Bible, when suddenly my glance became fixed as I beheld a man wearing a white robe-like garment, walking on the water in the direction parallel to where I was sitting. I watched Him as He proceeded to walk through the wall of my bedroom. I knew in my heart of hearts that this was Jesus, the Christ. Excited, I ran into the bedroom to greet and worship Him, but when I got there, I did not see Him.

With my heart still pounding in my chest, I sat on the bed, leaned against the headboard and pretended to read again. I say pretended because with such expectation in my heart, there was no way I could discern the words on the page I peered at. A few seconds later, all of my expectations were realized. He was there, sitting at the foot of the bed. I was frozen in time. My lips could not move so I couldn't speak. I sat there, eyes ablaze and my heart silently pleading and longing to touch the Master. The light of His countenance blotted out everything else in the room.

I stared until I was no longer looking upon Him; I was a part of Him. Suddenly, I was in what some would call another dimension, but in essence, I was in the Spirit. My flesh seemed to merge with the light and my mind drifted into a peace that truly surpassed understanding.

Then He spoke, *"Mary, I have called you unto Myself. I will teach you My Word and I will send you to My people. I will go into tradition and bring out the best and give them to you for training in My Word and My ways. They will become My disciples, and I will send you to the uttermost parts of the world to teach My people and turn their hearts back to Me. You will stand before dignitaries and heads of nations."*

Needless to say I was stuck back at "Mary". Regardless of the spelling on my birth certificate, the Lord knew me as Mary. He called my name, and was actually speaking to me. I felt the lips of my spirit as they began to slightly smile in amazement. His words were so personal and affirming, I knew that He was going to perform all that He spoke.

As He continued to speak, He told me how to start the ministry. He even told me the name of the radio broadcast (Bible Talk) that was to bring in some of those who would be helpers and workers of the vision. He spoke of holiness and godliness in ways that I had not heard ministered before. He also caused me to know that the true power of the Spirit could only be found in the humiliation of the flesh. I could write a book of several hundred pages to convey the details of the conversation, but then I have written many books and study guides which I have taught at Global Training Centers around the world. The revelations I have received are all being cataloged and made available in my Faith Library, *(www.marybanksfaithlibrary.com)*.

Jesus said, *"My people are not going to follow you; they are going to follow Me. If you have the guts to say what I say and to do what I do, then, I will bless you."* I cannot describe for you the joy, yet humility that I felt listening to His words. I knew He would be faithful to perform all that He purposed to do. But more than that, I knew all I had to do was obey. I remember Jesus saying to a congregation once: *...Verily, verily, I say unto you, The Son can do nothing of himself, but what he seeth the Father do: for what things soever he doeth, these also doeth the Son likewise. St. John 5:19* The vision was true to the Word. I knew I could trust it. Beloved, this removes the stress out of ministry and pleasing the Father: for truly my fellowship was with the Father and the Son.

Somehow I heard myself utter the words that had gathered in my heart. *"But Lord, I said. I don't love your people the way you do. I don't stay up all night praying for them. I go to sleep. I don't have the burden I need for prayer. Will you give me that burden? Will you teach me how to pray?"*

At that point He began to teach me the rudiments of prayer and led me into the travailing prayer that birthed the ministry gifts I now serve. That, of course, is another lesson. If you are struggling in prayer that seems to accomplish nothing, then seek out my book, ***"Lord, Teach Us to Pray."***

I think the most important thing I've learned from the Lord is the perspective of scripture and the true meaning of salvation. As I sit in my office and write this, I realize that it has been twenty-one years since that first visitation. You might wonder why it has taken so long to bring these truths to the Body. The answer is simple, I used to make television appearances on one of the larger Christian television networks. The saints in the church wanted to purchase some television time on that very network. They were quite "well-to-do" folk who were fascinated with the Word they heard.

They wanted the Body to hear the same. Just when all was set to go, the Lord spoke to me and said, *"If you go on the networks now, you will become another famous bible teacher without evidence of your message operating in the lives of My people. You will become sought after and embark on speaking engagements that will not afford you the time to raise My people in the Word I give you. Stay at home and develop Sons who will bring glory to My Father. Disciple them and make them strong in My ways. Raise up a body of believers who will not bring shame to My name."*

I obeyed the Lord, and remained in the quiver, listening and imparting the life He poured out to us. Subsequently, I received my commission; and this was the word God the Father spoke to me, as I lay prostrate on my bedroom floor. *"Even as I sent Moses into the land of Egypt to bring My people out of slavery, I am sending you to My Church to bring My people out of ignorance."* As we began to grow spiritually He increased my borders and added new measures to my territorial sphere of influence. In 1985 I began with twelve members/students, and now twenty-one years later we have founded works and developed Sons both here and abroad.

This is the reason I come to you now, with the first of many truths the Father has delivered to me. I am sure that there are others, like me, who have also been hidden in His quiver this many years. Be encouraged, the fact that the Father has allowed you to partake of these truths means that He is mindful of you and desires to use you in His service.

Chapter Two
YOU MUST BELIEVE AND AGREE

As I began to write this book I realized that my mind was being bombarded by the approved book writing protocol of our day. I found myself becoming nervous as to how I would present the message. But then I thought, "I have written over two hundred study guides and books that have been changing lives at Mary Banks Global Training Centers and Bible Teachers International Worship Centers for more than two decades. Now that we are introducing this Word to the Church at large, it is the same Word, presented in the same fashion that will perfect the Body."

I want you to follow me as I take you on a journey to the eternal purpose of God; the spiritual perfection of His Sons. In order to make this trip, however, you must meet the criteria the Father has set before us. ***You must agree that the holy Word of God is the authority that will settle <u>all</u> controversy.*** You must also open your heart to receive truth that may in fact shatter your present belief system.

St. John 7:38

> *He that believeth on me, <u>as the scripture hath said</u>, out of his belly shall flow rivers of living water,*

The living water Jesus speaks of here is the Holy Ghost. Jesus also said it is not that which goes into a man that defiles him, but that which comes forth out of him. The Lord implies that only those things pertaining to the Spirit of God will proceed from those who believe on Him according to the scriptures. This may seem very mundane to you, but I declare it is the number one problem in the Church today. Saints do not believe on Christ the way the scriptures have presented Him. Now your mind may go to His Coming or His crucifixion or maybe His return and you may say, *"Oh, yes, I do believe."* I do not speak here though of those events, I speak of His sojourning in you. It is His indwelling in your flesh and what that has afforded you that are the issues here. It is of those things that I speak concerning your unbelief.

I know of no other way to bring you to the place you seek in Him except you believe as the Word has proclaimed. The only weapon you have against the workings of a fleshy mind that has not been influenced by the purity of God's Word, is truth itself. It is that truth that will make you free from unlawful desires, mental anguish, hurts and sins of the flesh and mind.

Romans 12:1-2
> *1 I beseech you therefore, brethren, by the mercies of God, that ye present your bodies a living sacrifice, holy, acceptable unto God, which is your reasonable service.*
> *2 And be not conformed to this world: but be ye transformed by the renewing of your mind, that ye may prove what is that good, and acceptable, and perfect, will of God.*

Paul, the messenger of the Lord Jesus Christ and apostle to the church, infers here that the church at Rome can live in the presence of God and man without conforming to the way of the world. I am sure that you have heard these verses taught many times before. But what do they really mean? They imply that we are to be different in our ways and character.

There are many other scriptures that support this belief; passages such as: *"...what fellowship has righteousness with unrighteousness?" (II Corinthians 6:14)* or *"...love not the world, nor the things in the world," (I John 2:15)* or even *"ye are a peculiar people"(I Peter 2:9).* These all refer to a creature totally oblivious to the ways and things of the world. This is certainly not true with regard to the Sons of God today.

The Body of Christ is confused. The mind of the church has been consistently assailed by the traditions, isms and schisms of men. In fact there are many false doctrines that have systematically poisoned the people of God. The deadliest of these are the ***"Faith and Prosperity"*** and ***"Dual Nature"*** doctrines. These doctrines and traditions have created mindsets that totally contradict the eternal purpose of God. To say the least, they have perpetuated a lust for the things of this world and sin. They have fashioned a creature that is not even a facsimile of a real Son of God.

There has been much "to-do" about mindsets in the preaching of the gospel. According to *Webster's* dictionary, a "mindset" is a mental attitude or a fixed state of mind. Most of these discussions have done nothing more than confirm the great lie, which Satan has perpetrated in the church, ***"Nobody is Perfect."*** This declaration is the most horrid affront to the sacrifice of our Lord and Savior, Jesus Christ.

As an apostle to the Body of Christ, it is my responsibility to identify and destroy any mindset that exalts itself above the knowledge of God. There are many such teachings in the Body of Christ concerning the disposition of the mind that have grossly undermined the work of the cross.

First of all, the mind is not an evil thing in your body. According to scripture, it is the mechanism by which you are to serve the Lord. So then, how did it become the enemy of the soul? I submit to you that it is false doctrines and the erroneous teaching of salvation itself that have created this mental albatross for the saints of God. I too, was guilty of teaching such ignorance. It was the grace and mercy of God that stopped me in my tracks and set my feet on the path of knowledge and wisdom that changed my life and my ministry forever.

Let us take a look at the big picture for a moment. Depression, frustration, unforgiveness, jealousy, evil imagination etc., are all dispositions of the mind. They are merely manifestations of how the mind operates. Christianity has established spiritual psychiatric wards to deal with these ills. Thus, we have Christian psychiatry designed to walk the Sons of God through their spiritual deficiencies. Our counseling appointments have become therapeutic sessions in which the clergy spends most of its time trying to heal or change mental dispositions.

This is heresy! Listen to me carefully. When we the leaders in the Body of Christ, entreat depression, unforgiveness, hurts from offenses, evil imaginations and such dispositions as common defects in the children of God, we dishonor God and bring Christ to an open shame. I hope you will open your heart to hear what the Spirit is about to say to you.

Consider the following passages:
James 3:10-12

> *10 Out of the same mouth proceedeth blessing and cursing. My brethren, these things ought not so to be.*

11 Doth a fountain send forth at the same place sweet water and bitter?
12 Can the fig tree, my brethren, bear olive berries? either a vine, figs? so can no fountain both yield salt water and fresh.

Look at the **impossibilities** here. A fig tree cannot produce olives, nor does a fountain send forth salt and fresh water. You must accept the principle here. If olives are found on a tree it is because the tree is an olive tree. If a fountain produces salt water, it is because the source of the fountain is salt water.

The same is true of our walk in God. **God created each Son whole and complete, not emotionally crippled and wanton.** If we walk after the flesh we will mind the things of the flesh. Likewise, we will produce the character and emotions associated with the flesh. If we walk after the Spirit however, we will mind the things of the Spirit and engender the attributes and emotions of the Spirit of God. The bottom line is, **it is impossible to walk after the Spirit and produce the character and emotions of the flesh**.

Deep emotional pains, spiritual deficiencies, iniquity and wantonness are not attributes of the Spirit of God. In fact there is no captivity of the mind that is characteristic of a born-again believer who walks after the Spirit. It is impossible for the fig tree to produce olives.

What is the mindset here? Leadership in the Body has accepted the great lie. They believe that these "ills" will always exist in the Body of Christ and that there will always be defects in the born-again believer.

God is not an impotent God. He is mighty in all that He does and salvation is no exception. It is the mighty hand of God in the salvation of the Sons that is on trial here. Every time leaders in the Body entreat sin and emotional disorders such as depression, frustration, offenses and unforgiveness as conditions that the Father has raised up spiritual psychiatrists to deal with, they help to validate Satan's inference that God is an impotent God unable to keep that which He saved out of the world. If the Sons of God are victims of the same captivities as unbelievers then where is the power of their God?

I submit to you, it is the erroneous doctrines and perspectives regarding the born-again experience that is at the root of this controversy. In all the years that I have been a member of the Body of Christ, which are more than thirty, I have never really heard the gospel of Jesus Christ preached in its entirety. I have heard the message of a suffering servant and redeemer. I have read many books about the plight, the disposition and position of the Sons even as you have. We've heard many preachers proclaim the day of the manifested Sons of God. We marched through the Christian theatrics and fads; *"name it and claim it", "the king's kids", "step on the head of the devil",* and the most hilarious of them all, *"money...cometh".* We were even privileged to hear sermons exemplifying the fact that we can do all things through Christ.

But what was the bottom line? When the rubber met the road, we were still crippled by emotional pains, suppressing true desires and struggling to maintain righteous character on a daily basis. We went to conventions and conferences looking for the magic formula. We wanted to hear something that would end the struggle and cause us to walk in the power of the Holy Ghost. We knew enough to know that we were missing something, but because we didn't know what it was that we lacked, we continued to hunger and search for the knowledge or the prophecy or the laying on of hands that would finally catapult us into that long sought after place of power.

Most of us wanted to work ministry. So after long years of missing the mark and waiting for a *"power miracle,"* we left our seats of boredom and embarked on the trail of ministry that had been blazed by many who had the same frustrations. I had never heard the truth about His indwelling in us until the Lord revealed this awesome reality.

Do you really believe it is the heart and mind of God for His people to journey through life day after day trying to chart their path through a maze of false doctrines that promise but never really deliver? What about inner healing counseling that can only place bandages on our wounds, and sermons void of the power to perfect character? No wonder there is such hopelessness in the people of God. There have been so many messages of false hope delivered to them over the years, until the declaration that there are new voices with a new revelation coming to the forefront does very little to excite them. They have seen and heard too much. That is why the wisdom of God demanded that I remain at home with the flock until I produced the evidence of the truth I am sent to carry to the Body.

If I am not successful in making you understand the monumental principles, which are at the very core of your salvation, the writing of this book will have the same effect as putting a band-aid on a gunshot wound. You will have learned a few more truths without the power to execute them.

The key to power is the knowledge of God. It is the sure Word, pure and full of the purpose of God. It is not produced by doctrines devised as a result of the failure of men to walk in the righteousness of God. I know that your struggle to live holy and to be free from lingering hurts can be over if I can cause you to know the truth about the things God has freely given to His children. Stop for a moment and pray that clarity will come to your heart as you embark on this journey to the heart and mind of the Father.

THINGS WE MUST KNOW AND BELIEVE...

The scriptures insist that the Lord has given us things that can only be discerned by the Holy Ghost. It behooves us therefore to investigate these things that have been given to us freely by the Father who hath blessed us with all spiritual blessings in heavenly places in Christ...and that we should be holy and without blame *(Eph. 1:3,4)*.

We are a spiritual people, born of God and we have received a spiritual inheritance. The things the Father has given to us are in Christ. Christ is that unction, which John talked about in his epistle it, is the anointing. It is the Spirit of God that upholds all things and embodies all creation. Christ is a heavenly place. It is the omnipresence of God.

Though it is profitable for us to believe that the Father created us holy, strangely enough, this is the very truth the church has denied. The blessings He gave us that have been established to be spiritual blessings are simply the attributes of dwelling in Him.

The Father, has predestinated us unto **the adoption of children by Jesus Christ** to himself, according to the good pleasure of his will, to the praise of the glory of his grace, wherein he **hath made us accepted in the beloved** *(Eph. 1:5-6)*. Here Paul begins to explain the operation of redemption. He declares that we were to be more than beneficiaries of the atonement of Jesus Christ (as Israel benefited from the sacrifices of Moses). Instead we were elected and selected to become the children of God through Jesus Christ. **We must take this in the literal sense, we are the offspring of God**.

We have been placed in the royal family; **we are the begotten of God**. I remember the Lord saying in the book of St. John that Jesus was His beloved Son in whom He was well pleased. We have now been placed inside of that beloved Son. We are in Him and He is in us, even as Christ was in the Father and the Father was in Christ.

The problem here is that the church does not believe this literally. The church cannot believe and accept that we are the same creature possessing the same nature as Jesus Christ. Somehow we see Him as totally different . Many have not believed the report. They cannot believe that salvation allows us to be created in the likeness of the man Jesus Christ. Instead, they choose to camp out at the next verse.

We have redemption through his blood, and the forgiveness of sins, according to the riches of his grace (Eph. 1:7). The riches of God's grace establish His influence, which is the Holy Ghost within us. This placing of the Holy Spirit within, initiated a process of regeneration that transformed us into a New Creature.

Ephesians 3:3-5

> *3 How that by revelation he made known unto*
> *me the mystery; (as I wrote afore in few words,*
> *4 Whereby, when ye read, ye may understand*
> *my knowledge in the mystery of Christ)*
> *5 Which in other ages was not made known*
> *unto the sons of men, as it is now revealed unto*
> *his holy apostles and prophets by the Spirit;*

This is the mystery that was hid in God: the crucifixion of the old man; the creation of the New Creature; the begetting of Sons; and Christ in us, the hope of glory. These are the spiritual things that cannot be discerned by natural men because they are foolishness to them. The problem is the church has taken the same position as the natural man too, and does not believe. Even after having received the Spirit of Truth, the church continues to walk in denial of its inheritance.

I am convinced we have had only a partial revelation of the faith. Therefore, we have only had a partial revelation of our salvation. The church did not understand the dispensation of faith. Instead it packaged and commercialized faith as a commodity that guarantees a life of wealth and earthly power. Consequently, the Body has erred and strayed from the purpose of God. Therefore, neither the death of Christ, His resurrection, the forgiveness of sins, nor salvation for regeneration will have any effect on those who have become nonbelievers.

We must believe in the finished work of Christ. We must believe we are that which God has made us. If we do not believe that we are the Sons of God created in the image of Christ, there will be no evidence of the power of our salvation. We will never manifest Christ in these earthen bodies. This also means we will never walk in the character of Christ.

Belief is essential to our development. The New Creature must believe in who He is. We must believe that God has created us new. These are the things that the Holy Spirit has exposed, that we might know what the Father has done in us. This truth will remain ineffectual if we do not believe and accept it. The Father will deal with us no other way; we must simply believe that which the Holy Ghost teaches.

At some point in this study, you must accept the fact that **the true meaning of sonship is a perfect, sinless identity**. If not, you will never expect to live a life that is pleasing to the Father. You will always vacillate in and out of righteousness. You must believe on Christ the way that scripture has said.

There are many that have grown up in the Lord with me and we are the proof that you can live in this world free from sin and the crippling emotions Satan uses to ensnare the Sons. Continue to read and I will show you how to walk in the sinless perfection of our Lord Jesus Christ.

Chapter Three
THE MYSTERY

THE FELLOWSHIP OF THE MYSTERY

I am amazed at the excitement that I feel within each time I begin to teach on the mystery of Christ. In the more than thirty years I have been saved I have never heard a complete revelation of our salvation experience. This does not mean that the revelation has not been given to someone. It simply means that I have never heard it preached in a church, taught on television or read it in a book.

The word mystery does not occur in scripture until we reach the New Testament. In all but two of the scriptures where it is found, reference is made to the Mystery of Christ. The word *"mystery"* means **"a secret" or "to shut the mouth."** It is the hidden revelation of the work of the Father. This mystery of Christ remained hidden in God until the formation of the Church.

In this chapter I simply want to discuss the mystery itself. I want you to understand the knowledge in the mystery that was hid in God before the foundation of the world. By revelation, God has shown the mystery of Christ to me, and others, for this appointed time of reformation.

The mystery of Christ holds the key to the Sons of God fulfilling their call to righteousness. When Paul wrote to the church, he implied that they needed to understand the knowledge he had received concerning the mystery. **The mystery of Christ, the mystery of God** and the **mystery of**

Godliness are all the same. They can and are used interchangeably throughout the scripture.

Ephesians 3:9-10

> *9 And to make all men see <u>what is the fellowship of the mystery</u>, which <u>from the beginning of the world hath been hid in God</u>, who created all things by Jesus Christ:*
> *10 To the intent that now unto the principalities and powers in heavenly places might be known <u>by the church</u> the manifold wisdom of God,*

Revelation 10:7

> *But in the days of the voice of the seventh angel, when he shall begin to sound, <u>the mystery of God should be finished</u>, as he hath declared to his servants the prophets.*

We are about to discuss a secret that was hid in God before the beginning of the world. John, the Revelator saw the mystery finished at the sounding of the seventh trumpet or last trump. The events initiated by the blowing of the seventh trumpet revealed in the thirteenth and fourteenth chapters of Revelation culminate with the rapture of the Church. The apostle Paul also confirms the time of this event in his writings to the Corinthians.

I Corinthians 15:51-54

> *51 Behold, <u>I shew you a mystery</u>; We shall not all sleep, but we shall all be changed,*
> *52 In a moment, in the twinkling of an eye, at the last trump: for the trumpet shall sound,*

and the dead shall be raised incorruptible, and
we shall be changed.
53 For this corruptible must put on
incorruption, and this mortal must put on
immortality.
54 So when this corruptible shall have put on
incorruption, and this mortal shall have put on
immortality, then shall be brought to pass the
saying that is written, Death is swallowed up in
victory.

Paul has allowed us to conclude that this mystery of God is relative to the residency of the Sons of God on the earth. We know that the verses above describe the rapture of the Church. We are able to surmise, therefore that the mystery of God begins on the day of Pentecost and ends with the rapture of the Sons of God from the earth.

I am attempting to discuss this awesome feat of the Father in the most simplistic terms. I am glad to be able to talk about it without the formalities of a church or conference setting. Please allow me to casually discuss the secrets of our faith.

Firstly, we are the partakers of a plan that God did not reveal to anyone, until the Day of Pentecost. It is a mystery, a secret that He didn't even reveal to the angels until the time appointed. The text declares that none of the prophets of old were privy to the mystery. They were only given the promise of the coming Deliverer.

But what exactly is the mystery? What is this thing that was hidden? The mystery itself needs to be explained in simple terms that are confirmed by scripture.

THE PLAN

In order to save the man, who was dead (alienated from God), he must be taken out of the flesh which had become a walking coffin and be placed in the Spirit of Christ (which is the only life that exists) so that the walking coffin could become a living temple of God.

THE METHOD

The preaching of the gospel, which is the death, burial and resurrection of Jesus Christ, is the method God uses to bring man into fellowship with the mystery of Christ.

It is the plan and the method that makes the mystery. However, I think that most of the unbelief we experience is relative to the plan itself. Once you really look into the details of the plan, you will discover that the temple of God is the birthing of another Christ. This is what the Church does not believe. This has become my frustration with my ministry even as it was Paul's frustration with the church at Corinth.

This mystery that was hid from ages and generations is now made manifest (made known, revealed) to the saints. Not only did the Spirit reveal it to us, but we were also **made** the mystery by the same Spirit. Once again we ask, what is this mystery?

Colossians 1:27

> *To whom God would make known what is the riches of the glory of this mystery among the*

Gentiles; <u>which is Christ in you</u>, <u>the hope of glory</u>:

It was the intent of the Father to save this fallen race of man by what is called baptism; the submersion of believers into the Spirit of Christ. It is the taking of the inner man out of the flesh and placing him in the Spirit. The Spirit of God remained in the body hiding the individual in Christ who is in God.

Here we have the fallen sons of Adam whom God loves so much that He is not willing that they should perish. Their fall however, was not a surprise to Him because the plan for man's salvation was already formulated before the fall itself. God had condemned man to die naturally and spiritually as the penalty for sin. <u>So now salvation had to be for a people who were already under the captivity and dominion of sin and death.</u>

Romans 7:5

> *<u>For when we were in the flesh</u>, the motions of sins, which were by the law, did work in our members to bring forth fruit unto death.*

What does Paul mean by *"when we were in the flesh?"* Are we not in the same bodies as before we met the Lord? I think so. Then there has to be further explanation of this statement.

In Romans 7:5, Paul describes the state of an <u>unregenerate man</u>. To prove this point, as the 7th chapter of Romans is such a controversy in some schools of thought, you must read this passage in light of the following. This indicates a positional change: *<u>But ye are not in the flesh, but in the</u>*

Spirit, if so be that the Spirit of God dwell in you... (Romans 8:9).

At one point we were in the flesh. Our soul and spirit lived in the fleshy body without the presence or influence of God. But something happened to change our physical location. *For ye are dead, and your life is hid with Christ in God (Colossians 3:3).*

Paul's testimony of this positional change is even more compelling. *For in him we live, and move, and have our being; as certain also of your own poets have said, For we are also His offspring (Acts 17:28).* The inference here is that our spiritual or inward parts were physically placed in the Holy Ghost. This is what Paul means when he declares that we are not in the flesh. The spirit of man has been placed in Christ.

A most thorough description of this taking of the Adamic being out of the flesh is given to us in Paul's letter to the Romans. I have underlined the phrases that emphasize the nature of this baptism.

Romans 6:3-11

> *3 Know ye not, that so many of us as were baptized into Jesus Christ were baptized into his death?*
> *4 Therefore we are buried with him by baptism into death: that like as Christ was raised up from the dead by the glory of the Father, even so we also should walk in newness of life.*
> *5 For if we have been planted together in the likeness of his death, we shall be also in the likeness of his resurrection:*

6 Knowing this, that <u>our old man is crucified</u>
<u>with him</u>, that the body of sin might be
destroyed, that henceforth we should not serve
sin.
7 For he that is dead is freed from sin.
8 Now if <u>we be dead with Christ, we believe</u>
<u>that we shall also live with him</u>:
9 Knowing that Christ being raised from the
dead dieth no more; death hath no more
dominion over him.
10 For in that he died, he died unto sin once:
but in that he liveth, he liveth unto God.
11 Likewise <u>reckon ye also yourselves to be</u>
<u>dead indeed unto sin, but alive unto God</u>
<u>through Jesus Christ our Lord</u>.

It is imperative that you believe that which is written. <u>This is</u>
<u>the operation of God</u>. The living soul, which is the man
himself, was already dead (alienated from God). **The Father**
in His manifold wisdom and awesome power was able to
extract the soul from the flesh, place it in the Holy Ghost
and quicken the same body by the Spirit into a vessel of
righteousness, created unto good works. The baptism
into Christ is a fulfillment of the Promise God made to
Abraham. It was the Spirit that God promised him and his
seed. Look at this closely.

Galatians 3:14
> *That the blessing of Abraham might come on*
> *the Gentiles through Jesus Christ; that <u>we</u>*
> *<u>might receive the promise of the Spirit through</u>*
> *<u>faith</u>.*

The promise was the Spirit of God that was to be given to Jesus. As we can see from the verses above and below, the same Spirit was promised and given to us.

I Corinthians 3:16-17

> *16 Know ye not that ye are the temple of God, and that the Spirit of God dwelleth in you?*
> *17 If any man defile the temple of God, him shall God destroy; for the temple of God is holy, which temple ye are.*

I Corinthians 6:19-20

> *19 What? know ye not that your body is the temple of the Holy Ghost which is in you, which ye have of God, and ye are not your own?*
> *20 For ye are bought with a price: therefore glorify God in your body, and in your spirit, which are God's.*

You see, the church does not take these passages literally, or maybe I should say it has not comprehended the meaning to the extent that it would allow it to respond as true Sons of God. Even when the truth is revealed, it is not always or readily believed. This is heartbreaking because those in the Body of Christ already have the proof of the revelation within. Then too, it is the Spirit of God within them that bears witness of the truth. Why then do they not accept it as fact? I dare say it is because of their track record of failure in God. But as the scripture has proclaimed: *For what if some did not believe? shall their unbelief make the faith of God without effect? God forbid: yea, let God be true, but every man a liar; as it is written, That thou mightest be justified in thy sayings, and mightest overcome when thou art judged (Romans 3:3-4).*

Now back to the mystery. It is through Jesus Christ that this great unbelievable mystery would manifest. I like the way the Father spoke about it in the Old Covenant. In the last days I will do a "new thing." This meant He would do that which had never been done before, that, which the human mind could not conceive and which could only be discerned by His Spirit.

I Corinthians 2:9-10

> *9 But as it is written, Eye hath not seen, nor ear heard, neither have entered into the heart of man, the things which God hath prepared for them that love him.*
> *10 But God hath revealed them unto us by his Spirit: for the Spirit searcheth all things, yea, the deep things of God.*

My sister, my brother, the handiwork of God is awesome to behold. The mystery of Christ in us is manifested to the world by the riches of His glory. These are the things the old patriarchs did not see.

Chapter Four
DUAL NATURE: THE GREAT LIE

One of the most successful weapons of the enemy against the Church is the "Doctrine of Dual Nature." **"Dual" denotes the existence of two parts or elements: having a double character or nature.** *(Merriam-Webster Online Dictionary).*

The implication here therefore, is that the Sons of God have two natures; one of God, divine, and the other of the flesh, which can only be of Satan. If this is true then there is no hope for the Sons to ever come into the eternal purpose of God, which is for them to be conformed to the image of His first Son Jesus Christ. If the Sons of God are trapped inside of dual nature then the character of Satan, sins of the flesh, emotional trauma, and mental anguish will forever be the testimony of the Church. If this is the case, there is absolutely nothing that can be done except to adjust to these captivities and constantly repent for sin.

Many of the more prominent Bible teachers have made it a point to fervently minister this doctrine. They have thoroughly convinced millions of Christians that it is impossible for them to live a sinless life. These brethren are sincere in their quest to instruct the Body of Christ. However, the inference of such a doctrine is that God will never have a church that is holy, blameless, and without spot or blemish.

Hear me brethren, as I suggest that this doctrine was birthed in error due to a lack of understanding in the revelation of the mystery of Christ. If it is your desire to know the heart and mind of our Father, then give me this opportunity to expose the error of this doctrine. All I ask of you is that you allow the holy Word of God to be the authority and agree with what the scriptures have to say about this matter.

A. THEOLOGICAL THEORY

First of all, it is impossible to be 100% accurate when a doctrine is developed from observing the failure of men to produce God's purpose, as it is proclaimed in the Word. *For whom he did foreknow, he also did predestinate to be conformed to the image of his Son, that he might be the firstborn among many brethren (Romans 8:29).*

"To be conformed," means **to be fashioned like unto**. In composition it means *completeness*. The Father purposed or predetermined to fashion the Sons in the image of Christ. They are to be complete in Him, *lacking nothing*. The Lord ministered to me concerning the deception in the teachings that led to this perverted doctrine. He has shown me that it is a matter of perception regarding the indwelling Christ.   I hope to be able to articulate this error in a manner that illuminates the hearts and minds of those who are sincerely seeking the knowledge of God.

Where there is a general consensus that no one is walking in the perfection of Christ, or living a sinless life, it is easy for men to come up with a **scapegoat.** In this case it is the **flesh**. It has been concluded that the fact that we are in this human body makes it impossible for us to live a holy existence 24 hours a day, 7 days a week. Thus, we have a doctrine that was born out of failure.

In order for the doctrine to appear meaningful however, the failure cannot be considered a failure; it must become a "non-expectation". **In other words, if a saint does not live a perfected life, it is not because he failed, it is because he was never "expected" to do so.** It must follow then that it was not the intent of God to create a Son who was altogether free from sin. Instead he is merely the same man, essentially a sinner who has now accepted Jesus Christ as a shield that protects him from the wrath of God that will come upon unbelievers.

In this theory, the blood of Jesus merely covers our sin and the Spirit of Christ is only the seed or seal that identifies us as one who has accepted Jesus. Although we teach the attributes of Christianity as written in the Word, such as the Ten Commandments, the Beatitudes, etc., apparently God never expected us to fulfill those laws and attributes on a daily basis. At some point, He knew that we would sin, so He made Jesus Christ our advocate and intercessor.

If the Lord never intended or expected the Sons to be sinless in their walk here on earth, then the fact that the scriptures imply we have taken on the divine nature, does not allow for the presence of the lower nature of the flesh. **This means that flesh was not in the least bit affected by the salvation experience.** The two things that stand to support this theory are:

- These are the same bodies we had before salvation.
- These bodies commit sin against the Lord.

All of this seems so matter of fact. It all seems like the perfect explanation for the spiritual condition of the Body of Christ, but it is all fiction; there is no God-defined purpose in this theory. It is the most blatant undermining of the purpose of God that we could ever experience.

Millions of Christians have been made privy to this gross misrepresentation of God and His plan for man. It has robbed them of the very hope of being able to please the Father in their daily walk. *It has bred an expectation to sin and dishonor the Lord.* It is no surprise that Christians suffer from frustration, depression, lust, hurt and un-forgiveness. Although some people measure sin in degrees of severity, each time we sin, we put Him to an open shame. Now that the foundation for the error has been established, let us see what God's real intentions were.

B. THE TRUTH ABOUT SALVATION

An understanding of the salvation experience is what has eluded many ministers of the gospel. After all, <u>this is the mystery</u> that was hid in God before the foundation of the world: *Christ in you the hope of glory (Colossians 1:27).* This mystery was revealed to the apostles first and then to the holy prophets for confirmation. It is now given to the church through apostolic order without deviation. The church has been mandated to continue steadfastly in the apostles' doctrine. If an angel or any other creature teaches any doctrine other than that which was, and is, being revealed to God's apostles, it is to be a curse to him. We will discuss this further in a later chapter.

The key to understanding the mystery of godliness is to understand what happened in the Garden of Eden. We know that Adam and Eve were created innocent. God gave them a commandment, wherein He forbade them to touch or eat of the "Tree of the Knowledge of Good and Evil." He warned them saying, *"But of the tree of the knowledge of good and evil, thou shalt not eat of it: for in the day that thou eatest thereof thou shalt surely die" (Genesis 2:17).* Eventually they did eat, throwing the whole human race into the captivity of sin and death.

I am going to go through a barrage of scriptures that will show the awesome power of God, as He worked His purpose in redemption. Please open your heart and follow me into a spiritual revelation that will change your life and your ministry. Consider each of the facts as to whether or not they are adequately supported by scripture, or whether the scriptures contradict them. This method of examination of a teaching is fair and totally acceptable by the Holy Spirit. Besides, it is what I did with the doctrine of *"Dual Nature,* (it does not stand the test of all scripture; therefore, it cannot be the Word of God.)

ADAM SINNED BY CHOICE

Before the fall Adam was sinless in nature and in deed. He lived a perfect, sinless life on a daily basis. There was no struggle in him to abide in righteousness. There was no driving force within compelling him to disobey. Adam succumbed to temptation outside of the body. He was **willingly** seduced by his wife. According to Paul, Adam was not deceived. He made a sober-minded decision to disobey his God.

These facts ought to make you stop and consider that God was able to make a man who did not have the indwelling of the Holy Ghost; yet He demanded and expected that he live a perfect, sinless life forever. That's right. God expected and even commanded Adam to live a sinless life forever and ever.

Before we go any further, I can hear someone saying, "But wait a minute, Adam did have the Spirit of God in him." To remove all the controversy concerning this issue, let us allow the scriptures to do what they do best.

I Corinthians 15:45-48

45 And so it is written, The first man Adam was made a living soul; the last Adam was made a quickening spirit.
46 <u>Howbeit that was not first which is spiritual, but that which is natural; and afterward that which is spiritual.</u>
47 The first man is of the earth, earthy: the second man is the Lord from heaven.
48 As is the earthy, such are they also that are earthy: and as is the heavenly, such are they also that are heavenly.

Did you note the distinctions Paul makes between the two Adams? The first is a living soul, natural (of nature) and earthy. The second is a quickening spirit, spiritual and heavenly. As we have borne and walked in the image and disposition of the first, now we shall walk in the mind of the second.

Jesus said, "That which is born of flesh is flesh and that which is born of the spirit is spirit." *Furthermore we have had fathers of our flesh which corrected us, and we gave them reverence: shall we not much rather be in subjection unto the Father of spirits, and live? (Heb 12:9).* Sooner or later you must come to the place where you accept the fact that we, who are born of God, are spiritual beings. We are another race on the planet that is neither black nor white. We are new creatures, the Sons of the Most High God.

If it had been impossible for Adam and his offspring to keep the commandments of God, then God would not have installed the penalty of condemnation as a consequence for disobedience. God is just and righteous in all His judgments. Why then is it so impossible to believe that He could birth offspring through a second sinless Adam, (one who has His Spirit), and expect them to live a sinless life? [I want you to keep this in mind as we continue to expose the truth about salvation.]

THE WORKS OF THE DEVIL: SIN, DEATH & CAPTIVITY

The human spirit was free from sin before the fall of Adam. It knew no sin neither did it crave sin. There was no evil concupiscence working in the members of its body. Adam disobeyed God however, and when he did, the spirit of Satan, which Paul calls the spirit of iniquity, took possession of the human spirit. It was this seed of Satan living and breeding in the human race that caused it to fall into darkness and despair.

And God saw that the wickedness of man was great in the earth, and that every imagination of the thoughts of his heart was only evil continually. And God looked upon the earth, and behold, it was corrupt; for all flesh had corrupted his way upon the earth (Gen. 6:5, 12). The question worth asking is, "What caused flesh to become so corrupt and hideous in the earth?" It was the indwelling of the spirit of bondage and captivity. Jesus addressed this in His discourse with the scribes and Pharisees, *"You are of your father, the devil, and it is his lusts you will do" (St. John 8:44).* And *"I speak that which I have seen with my Father: and ye do that which ye have seen with your father" (St. John 8:38).*

In His very first sermon, Jesus declared that He had come to *preach deliverance to the captives*, *(St. Luke 4:18). For this purpose the Son of God was manifested, that He might destroy the works of the devil (I John 3:8).*

After sin entered the world, all who came from the seed of Adam came under the captivity of sin and death. *Wherefore, as by one man sin entered into the world, and death by sin; and so death passed upon all men, for that all have sinned: (Romans 5:12).* **The human body became the body of sin.** Sin was in its conception, thus providing it with a sin nature. The testimony of the psalmist is that he was *"born in sin and in iniquity his mother did conceive him" (Psalm 51:5).*

In times past we walked according to the course of this world, according to the prince of the power of the air, the spirit that now worketh in the children of disobedience: Among whom also we all had our conversation in times past in the lusts of our flesh, fulfilling the desires of the flesh and of the mind; and were by nature the children of wrath, even as others (Eph. 2:2-3).

You must accept that in the fall of man there was an occupation. THE SPIRIT OF DARKNESS ACTUALLY LIVED IN MAN. It was this spirit living in man that changed his nature from one of innocence to one of sin. Once again, the important thing that should not be missed here is that the indwelling of a foreign spirit provided a new and sinful nature for the human race.

Paul reminds also that in times past, we were by nature children of wrath, even as others. In other words, before we received Christ, we were of the same nature as those who have never accepted Him. Due to the sinful nature of man, Jesus was able to make this statement to the scribes and Pharisees. *Ye are of your father the devil, and the lusts of your father ye will do. He was a murderer from the beginning, and abode not in the truth, because there is no truth in him. When he speaketh a lie, he speaketh of his own: for he is a liar, and the father of it (St. John 8:44).*

Jesus declared that <u>Satan had become the father of the human race</u>, and <u>his lust is what worked in the flesh</u>. In conclusion, the devil created a race of beings that were no longer subject to the laws of God. They took on the character and attributes of their father, Satan thus man became a liar, a murderer as well as an enemy of God.

THE LAW OF SIN

SATAN WAS IN CONTROL OF MAN COMPLETELY: BODY, SOUL AND SPIRIT. The strong man had gained control of the human spirit and rendered him helpless to the law of sin in his flesh. *For I delight in the law of God after the inward man: But I see another law in my members, warring against the law of my mind, and bringing me into captivity <u>to the law of sin which is in my members</u> (Romans 7:22-23).*

THE EFFECT OF THE SPIRIT OF INIQUITY LIVING IN MAN WAS EVIL CONCUPISCENCE IN THE FLESH. The presence of the spirit of darkness in man did not leave him with a choice regarding sin. He was completely and thoroughly under the control of the ***spirit of iniquity*** - the strong man abiding within. *But sin, taking occasion by the commandment, <u>wrought in me all manner of concupiscence</u>. For without the law sin was dead (Romans 7:8).*

The common thread here is *concupiscence*. It is more than occasional lust. **According to Strong's Concordance, "concupiscence" is a continual longing for those things God has forbidden.** This was the consequence of eating from the Tree of the Knowledge of Good and Evil. Lust for the things of this world now began to work in the members of the body. *For when we were in the flesh, the motions of sins, which were by the law, did work in our members to bring forth fruit unto death (Romans 7:5).*

<u>**This is the law of sin: evil concupiscence.**</u> It is emotions, influence and affection for sin continually working in the members of the body. Remember, Eve saw the fruit to be pleasant (lust of the eyes), good for food (lust of the flesh), and desirable to make one wise (the pride of life) *(I John 2:16)*. <u>The law of sin created continual lust in the flesh that could never be quenched.</u>

The law of sin brought man's flesh into captivity. This evil could not be overcome by will power alone because the corruption within had corrupted the flesh. *For when we were in the flesh, the <u>motions of sins</u>, which were by the law, did work in our members to bring <u>forth fruit unto death</u> (Romans 7:5).*

But is this our testimony having now been born again by the Spirit of God? <u>Were we reborn with the same sinful nature that characterized us as children of wrath</u>? This is where there is a parting of the minds. Some theologians have erred here in their revelation of salvation. They have carried this evil concupiscence into the salvation experience.

Were we reborn into the Body of Christ with dual or two natures? If so, then it is indeed impossible to live free from sin. It is amazing how the Body has accepted the fact that we are free from death in that we have inherited eternal life. Yet it simply refuses to accept that the Spirit, which gave us eternal life, is the self-same Spirit that has given us freedom from the bondage of sin.

CHRIST'S BODY

It might be easier to understand if we first look into the method, which is Jesus Christ. We know that the Holy Ghost overshadowed Mary and placed the seed of God in her womb. <u>Mary supplied the seed with a body</u> and the body that she provided became the body of Christ. That was a human body and so He could be called the "man" Jesus. The "body" is the only thing then that made Him a relative of the human race. What do we really have here? A one hundred percent human body, filled with the Holy Ghost. **Thus Jesus is the "man," and Christ is the "God in the man." It is the seed of God that provided Jesus' body with divine nature, but it was His submission to the Spirit that dwelled within Him that made Him holy and acceptable unto the Father**.

<u>It is also the Spirit of God within the body who quickened that human flesh and made it alive unto God and godliness</u>. **Without the Holy Ghost, that body would have been like any other human, susceptible to the Law of Sin and Death**. <u>Because of the indwelling of the Spirit however, and the obedience of the man to the will of the Father, the body itself remained sanctified unto God</u>. **My point here is that Jesus Christ was made like unto us, or rather; we have been made like unto Him in that we are now partakers of His flesh**.

Ephesians 3:6

> *That the Gentiles should be fellowheirs, <u>and of</u> <u>the same body</u>, and partakers of his promise in Christ by the gospel:*

Ephesians 5:29-30

> *29 For no man ever yet hated his own flesh; but nourisheth and cherisheth it, even as the Lord the church:*
> *30 For <u>we are members of his body</u>, of his flesh, and of his bones.*

The Holy Ghost anointed the body that Jesus lived in therefore, He is called Christ. His body was the temple of God. It is the same Spirit of Christ who inhabits our bodies. There is only one Spirit who occupies many bodies. We all have the self-same Spirit within, providing us with the same divine nature. That makes us all the body of Christ. We have become His flesh and His bones.

THE SEED OF GOD <u>CHANGED THE NATURE</u> OF THE NEW CREATURE. In spite of what you may have believed, you must stay with scripture.

II Peter 1:4

> *Whereby are given unto us exceeding great and precious promises: that by these <u>ye might be partakers of the divine nature</u>, having escaped the corruption that is in the world through lust.*

I Peter 1:23

> *Being born again, not of corruptible seed, but of incorruptible, by the word of God, which liveth and abideth for ever.*

I John 3:9

> *Whosoever is born of God doth not commit sin; for his seed remaineth in him: and he cannot sin, because he is born of God.*

No beloved, we no longer have the Adamic nature. We are born of the seed of God. We are His children and as such we are partakers of His divine sinless nature. He did not give us the Spirit of bondage again *(Romans 8:15)*.

Once again I can hear the skeptic saying, "Wait a minute Mary, you need to stop and consider that our flesh has known and experienced sin and that is the difference in comparison to Jesus Christ. He never committed sin, therefore it is logical to conclude that He had a sinless nature, which allowed Him to live a sinless life." As always these issues can be resolved by the prudence of God's wisdom consider the following passages.

II Corinthians 5:21

> *For he hath made him to be sin for us, who knew no sin; that we might be made the righteousness of God in him.*

Isaiah 53:6

> *...and the LORD hath laid on him the iniquity of us all.*

Here we have the man Jesus, who did no sin but definitely became sin by taking upon His body the sins of the whole world. There was and is no sin that was foreign to Him, He bore them all. Follow the Spirit here as we peer into the mind of the Father. Christ was innocent and He committed no sin during His walk here on earth. On the way to the cross however, He took on my sin, your sin and that of us all. Remember, He did not just die for the sins of the world: He actually carried our sin in His body, *Having abolished in his flesh the enmity...(Eph. 2:15)*. It was because of the sin *we did esteem him stricken, smitten of God, and afflicted (Isa. 53:4).*

Now I ask you, did Jesus make a conscious decision to take on the sins of the world or not, knowing that this would cause Him to be separated from God and to suffer the penalty of death and hell? No, He didn't commit sin, but He certainly chose to become sin for our sake. The penalty for such a choice was death and hell, and He submitted to both. But on the third day the Father retrieved His Son from the jaws of hell and declared, *"Thou art my Son, this day have I begotten thee."* We must consider the first part of the verse here as well; *God hath fulfilled the same unto us their children, in that he hath raised up Jesus again; as it is also written in the second psalm, Thou art my Son, this day have I begotten thee (Acts 13:33).* And now add to this, John's discourse from his vision on the Isle of Patmos, *"Jesus Christ, who is the faithful witness, and the first begotten of the dead, . . . (Rev 1:5).*

The bottom line is: Jesus was begotten again from the dead. After dying because of sin, he was raised or rather begotten again as the Son of God. Even after having become sin, He was raised the righteousness of God, with the nature of God.

But look at this, He was the first begotten from the dead. We are also begotten again from the dead, by the same Spirit that raised Christ (*I Peter 1:3*). Why then is it so hard to accept that we also were raised the righteous, sinless divine nature of God? We are His offspring, how could we have anything less than a sinless identity?

Furthermore, we often speak of the sinless identity of Jesus Christ because even though Mary provided Him with a human body, He was born of God and not man. The same is true of us, even though we live in an earthen vessel, *as many as received him, to them* (to us) *gave he power to become the sons of God, even to them* (to us) *that believe on his name: which were born,* (we were born)*, not of blood, nor of the will of the flesh, nor of the will of man, but of God (St. John 1:12-13).*

I want you to consider this; if the seed of the devil in Adam and all his offspring could produce children of wrath, how much more should the seed of God, which remains in us, produce the fruits of righteousness?

At salvation the Lord set a new law in motion and that is the Law of the Spirit of Life. This change of nature included the flesh. Beloved you are only one person. Don't accept a doctrine that divides you into two people. Your body is a part of your being and it too belongs to God. *For ye are bought with a price: therefore glorify God in your body, and in your spirit, which are God's (I Corinthians 6:20).*

This theory of a dual nature is void of choice. Man has to blame someone or something for his own disobedience to the Father. The flesh with its history of sin is an easy fall guy, but this is not the reality of grace. The sin nature along with its affections, emotions and influences were done away with at salvation and the next chapter will prove that.

Chapter Five
THE CIRCUMCISION OF FLESH

Theologians have concluded that the body (flesh) was not included in any way in the salvation process. Maybe they never really considered that the whole man had to die in order to be reborn. Because they proclaimed that the flesh has been excluded from the salvation experience, it was easy to conclude that the flesh is still and will always be under the captivity of the law of sin.

However, the Father did not neglect to deal with the flesh in the salvation process. **He knew that the Law of Sin and Death working in the members (the flesh) would once again bring us into captivity.** As we allow the Word to express itself without any private interpretation, open your heart to the possible assassination of your belief system.

In writing to the church at Colosse, Paul declared, *"ye are complete in Him" (Col. 2:10).* This means we are lacking in nothing. It also means the work of the devil is destroyed and nothing else has to be done. We don't need to receive anything else to accomplish that which God has called us to do and to be. The Father has given us all things that pertain to His life and godliness. When we say we are deficient, we can only be deficient in those things He told us to add to our faith *(II Peter 1:5-7).* God's work is finished.

Colossians 2:11-12
> *11 In whom also ye are circumcised with the circumcision made without hands, in putting off the body of the sins of the flesh by the circumcision of Christ:*

12 Buried with him in baptism, wherein also ye are risen with him through the faith of the operation of God, who hath raised him from the dead.

As it relates to salvation, our **error** came when we only saw the regeneration of the new man from within. *"**Circumcision**"* in the natural is *a cutting away of the foreskin from the male genitals.* Spiritual circumcision is also a cutting away, a sanctifying and cleansing of the flesh. **It is an operation of God wherein He cut away or removed from us the dominion of sin. It is God who put off from us the body of sin.**

When the old man was slain (crucified with Christ) at salvation, God placed the soul and the spirit in the Holy Ghost. But the same Holy Ghost also quickened our mortal bodies and brought us alive unto God. **We rose complete in Christ.** The Father has taken away all our excuses. **Our flesh is no longer the body of sin but has truly become the body of Christ.**

Let us allow the scriptures to take us further into this magnificent operation of God.

I Thessalonians 5:23
> *And the very God of peace sanctify you WHOLLY; and I pray God your whole spirit and soul and body be preserved blameless unto the coming of our Lord Jesus Christ.*

From the time we are born-again until the return of Jesus, our body, soul and spirit should be free from sin. Some of my brothers contend that this is impossible. You have to decide which you are going to believe, the scriptures or the vain philosophy of men. *For what the law could not do, in that it was weak through the flesh, God sending his own Son in the likeness of sinful flesh, and for sin, condemned sin in the flesh (Romans 8:3).*

The finished work of Christ condemned sin in the flesh. What would be the purpose of even writing such a Word if the Sons of God were doomed to be locked in a daily struggle with the law of sin in the flesh? This is as oil and water the two just don't mix. God made provisions for us to live a holy, sinless life here on earth. The law was unable to do so, but the circumcision of the flesh through Jesus Christ has destroyed the power and dominion of sin within and without. Paul declares that we were sanctified wholly or completely; body, soul and spirit. This is the work and Word of God. *And you, being dead in your sins and the uncircumcision of your flesh, hath he quickened together with him, having forgiven you all trespasses (Colossians 2:13).*

The sin issue was dealt with at salvation. God removed the dominion of sin in the baptism "into Christ," we rose in the body of Christ. The truth is, if sin is an issue it is because we, as Sons of God, make a conscious decision to sin against the Father. We do this in spite of the great love and mercy He has shown us. We now have the mind of Christ and are able to receive the following instructions and commandments. *That every one of you should know how to possess his vessel in sanctification and honour; Not in the lust of concupiscence, even as the Gentiles which know not God (I Thessalonians 4:4-5).* We were unable to do this before, because the nature of the flesh was that of evil concupiscence and we could not help ourselves. We are now instructed to possess our vessels in the sanctification the Father has provided. <u>We have overcome the lust of concupiscence that worked in our members</u> and are now instructed to possess our vessels.

The law could not stop sin in the flesh because it was the nature of the flesh to sin. You cannot teach a cat to bark and act like a dog because that is not his nature. It was impossible to live free from sin without the indwelling of the Spirit of God, which provided a new life and nature for the whole man. Christ is not merely a shield to protect us from the wrath of God. **He is our life**. He is the life we live right now. It is by Him that we live and move and it is by His faith that we are able to please the Father. Our life is hid in Him and He is that hidden treasure in us; ...*as he is, so are we in this world* (I John 4:17).

To live a life vacillating in and out of sin is to <u>live a lie</u>. It is not the nature of the Sons of God to live in any sin. To do so is to dishonor God and undermine the work of the Holy Ghost in us. A sinner is **not** who you are. In spite of how the songwriter has portrayed the Sons of God, we are **not** sinners who fall down and get up. We are the righteousness of God created in the image of Christ Jesus. <u>We are divine in nature and have overcome the corruption of the world</u> through lust of the flesh.

To say we have a dual nature because of our ability to sin against the Father is to say that Jesus Christ was completely incapable of disobeying the Father. If that is true, then His temptation in the wilderness and all the trying and testing He withstood was merely a show, considering He could not sin anyway. That would make Him out to be a fraud, for how could He be tempted in all points like unto us, if it was impossible for Him to sin in the first place? <u>Yes, He could</u>

have disobeyed, He simply chose not to. We have the same choice.

Consider Paul's instructions to Timothy. *All scripture is given by inspiration of God, and is profitable for doctrine, for reproof, for correction, for instruction in righteousness:* ***That the man of God may be perfect, thoroughly furnished unto all good works*** (*II Timothy 3:16-17*). The Word of God was given to keep us in the boundaries of the faith. We can be perfect, whether some believe it or not.

Chapter Six
THE EMOTIONS OF THE SPIRIT

When tradition told us we would never be one hundred percent holy as long as we lived in these bodies of flesh we believed that report. The general consensus was that the flesh was sinful and sooner or later it would cause us to sin against God. The reason we believed it was because we were witnesses first hand to the sinful track record of the Sons even after salvation. This may sound harsh but it is true nevertheless. Sin in the Body of Christ has caused us to believe it is impossible to live a perfected life before God.

But what about the script that says, *"the motions of sin" which worked in our members to bring about fruit unto death?* I really want to take time here to hover over this point. If you were to look up the term "motions" in Strong's Concordance you would find that it refers to emotions, affections and influence. Therefore the inference here is that when we were in the flesh, (unsaved, void of the Spirit of God), sin in our members produced emotions or affections that were the fruits of death. *Now the works of the flesh are manifest, which are these; Adultery, fornication, uncleanness, lasciviousness, Idolatry, witchcraft, hatred, variance, emulations, wrath, strife, seditions, heresies, Envyings, murders, drunkenness, revellings, and such like: of the which I tell you before, as I have also told you in time past, that they which do such things shall not inherit the kingdom of God (Galatians 5:19-21).*

Every captivity of the mind has its root in one of these works of the flesh. These are the emotions, influence and affections of a sin and death nature. When we were in the flesh these were the emotions we produced according to the Law of Sin and Death working in our members. I need you to see that these negative emotions and affections should only be brought forth by one who is unsaved, not influenced and void of God and godliness. Don't forget, the fig tree does not produce olives!

Please allow me to reiterate. These are the emotions or affections of the flesh that are produced by those who either do not know God or those who know Him but decide to walk after the way of the world. *But ye are not in the flesh, but in the Spirit, if so be that the Spirit of God dwell in you (Romans 8:9).* If we are now in the Spirit, then should it not follow that our emotions and affections be that of the Spirit? *But the fruit of the Spirit is love, joy, peace, longsuffering, gentleness, goodness, faith, Meekness, temperance: against such there is no law. And they that are Christ's have crucified the flesh with the affections and lusts. If we live in the Spirit, let us also walk in the Spirit (Galatians 5:22-25).*

According to the above scripture, those who are born of Christ have indeed crucified the affections and lusts of the flesh. If the above scripture is the truth and the affections (emotions) and lust of the flesh were crucified at salvation, then we are indeed free. Beloved, this is something the Father did. This is the work of faith, the operation of God. You will learn more about that in the next chapter.

I beg to differ with my distinguished colleagues who are yet to come into the full revelation of the Christ within. The fruit of the Spirit are not just subjects for missionaries to develop 15-minute "sermonettes" about. They are the attributes, affections, emotions and influence of the Holy Ghost in the flesh. It is the flesh that is gentle, full of joy and love when the Son walks according to who and what he is.

In turn, they are the attributes and emotions of the manifested Sons of God.

One very prominent Bible teacher maintains that we will continue to struggle with the sin nature of the flesh until Jesus returns or we simply die. Though I am sure my brother means well, this is simply not the truth. In fact, it is a heretical doctrine that undermines and even dishonors the work our Father performed at salvation.

The body you are in is **not** evil. It can do nothing you do not tell it to do. You are in control of your flesh. That is what your freedom from captivity is all about. You are able to choose good or evil. Your body is the temple of the Holy Ghost. You are instructed to present it holy and acceptable unto God, but this is impossible if the nature of the body is that of sin. The sin nature is enmity against God. It is not subject to God and neither can it ever be. Knowing this, the Lord sanctified the flesh in regeneration.

When theologians insist that the motions of sin were never taken out of the flesh by the Father they are coming up short in their revelation of the work of the cross. Furthermore, if we are the ones who have to crucify and cast out the old man, then, where is the work of grace and at what point did salvation set the captives free?

It is a fact that one day we will receive our spiritual bodies, but until then it is with the mind of this body that we will serve the Lord. The mind is the spirit of the flesh. If the nature of the flesh has not changed then it is impossible to renew its mind. As one of my esteemed colleagues points out, the nature of sinful flesh cannot be improved. Believe it or not, God also knew it was impossible. Therefore,

According as his divine power hath given unto us all things that pertain unto life and godliness, through the knowledge of him that hath called us to glory and virtue (II Peter 1:3).

Chapter Seven
PUTTING FAITH IN PERSPECTIVE

Please do not see this as just another "faith and prosperity" message that promises you the wealth of this world. There is no such promise in the Bible for the **Church** of the Lord Jesus Christ; none, at least not in the sense that we have been taught. Here we will go directly to the mind of the Lord concerning this matter of faith. Beloved, having been in the presence of the Lord, I cannot wait to share with you the astounding things He has spoken to me concerning this matter.

I hope you also feel a sense of urgency as the signs of the end times are upon us. The **Church** must be taught the truth and be prepared to deal with a world of hostility and hatred of God. This is the only way we will be molded into the image of our Savior, prepared for the battle ahead and reign victoriously in the end. The victory that the **Church** is to experience will be manifested in its ability to glorify Jesus in the midst of persecution, sin and afflictions.

This is so serious! Why? Because you probably are even as I was. You have held fast to the "faith and prosperity" teachings of our mainstream television and conference evangelists. These "name it, claim it," "confess it and possess it, and money cometh" rituals we learned over the years have left us totally frustrated and weary in our well doing.

We were babies, ready to eat and digest anything that sounded like the Word of God. We did not know that the very food we cherished so much was the greatest dose of spiritual poison we could have swallowed. We have been systematically poisoned over these years of learning and this is why the spiritual growth of the Body has been stunted. Notice I said spiritual growth has been stunted, not the size of the Body of Christ. Yes, the **Church** has grown in numbers. However, there is a serious problem in the spiritual disposition of the **Church**. We have become a greedy, self-seeking, self-serving, gainsaying people. The wantonness of the flesh has controlled the movement of the **Church** for years and man's doctrines have been installed to feed that lust and to prey upon God's inheritance.

We are divided on basic Bible doctrines, and as a result, we are fragmented and "denominationalized". There are wars and disputes causing schisms in the **Body**. Traditions and doctrines of men have become successful at making the Word of God of none effect.

Ask yourself these questions. "How could the enemy be so successful in neutralizing the power of the **Church**? How was he able to cause the saints of God to begin to think, feel and act like the world? How could he have almost totally destroyed the manifestation of any distinction between the Body of Christ and the world? What was his weapon?"

Satan's use of the Word of God, through the "Faith and Prosperity" message infiltrated the **Church** with erroneous doctrines, teachings and mindsets that utterly contradict Christ's teachings of self-denial, ordained suffering and patience. It is true that devout men and women of God who really believed in what they preached taught these messages. You can be certain, however, that at some point in these individuals' lives, the Holy Spirit tried or will try to reach them with the truth.

I recall a ministerial colleague saying, "Oftentimes we are caught, even trapped, inside of our own pet belief systems." This is so true. It can become very difficult to retract teachings that have sold thousands, even millions, of books and tapes. It can become even more difficult to go back to an audience of millions to say, "I've been wrong in my teachings all these years."

This is not to say that everything we were taught by our forefathers was error, not in the least. What I am trying to say is this:

1.   Much of the teachings we received had many truths contained in them, nevertheless the perspective from which they were taught had been wrong. The Faith and Prosperity message is one such teaching in which the saints of God must contend with the devil for earthly wealth and self-exaltation. Although we may find many truths in these teachings, they are indeed not "The Truth."

2.   Consider; if the Body had been exposed to the whole truth, how that truth would remove the wars, the schisms and the disunity of the Body. Why? Simply because we would all be speaking the same thing.

I Corinthians 1:10
>   *Now I beseech you, brethren, by the name of our Lord Jesus, that ye all speak the same thing, and that there be no divisions among you, but that ye be perfectly joined together in the same mind and in the same judgment.*

In this and other chapters I will go straight to the heart of the matter in the hope of providing you with another perspective to studying God's Word. If you are not earnestly moved to investigate in much more detail the nature of the Biblical teachings on the Dispensation of Faith, then indeed I will have failed in my attempt to bring more of the grace of God into your life.

Allow me to do this and I trust you will never be the same. You will read the Bible differently, you will see into the mind and heart of the Father and you will see yourself differently as well. You will be moved to purify yourself, enabling you to be used in the Master's plan.

Remember, I used to believe in, teach and respond to the same message you may be receiving now. We all preached what we were taught. When the Lord visited me with this revelation of Faith, the first thing I did was to go to my congregation and say to them, "I was wrong! The Lord has instructed me more perfectly on the operation of faith." There is no shame in this. Believe me brothers and sisters, the Body of Christ will love and respect you even more.

I was called to be an apostle of the Lord Jesus Christ and instructed to teach the Body of Christ the mysteries of the Kingdom of God. Truly, I can say it was the revelation of Faith that initially changed my life and my ministry.

As Paul explains, these mysteries were hidden from men in other ages or dispensations. We need to look more closely at the term "dispensation". Some Bible dictionaries do not agree that a *dispensation* in the script is **a period of time.** But, not only is it a period of time, it is also **the method of**

management, administration or stewardship extended by God within this certain time frame. For example:

The Dispensation of the Law (The Ten Commandments and its ordinances) began with Moses and ended with Jesus.

The Dispensation of Grace and Truth (The mystery of God) began with Jesus Christ and will end with the Rapture of the Church *(Revelation 10:7)*. It is also the dispensation of "Faith".

But now that which was hid in God is made known to the Church by the apostles of His Son, Jesus Christ. This next verse tells us specifically what the mystery of God is…

Colossians 1:27
> *To whom God would make known what is the riches of the glory of this <u>mystery among the Gentiles; which is Christ in you, the hope of glory</u>:*

The mystery that was hid in God throughout the ages and generations of men is that the time would come when "Christ" the anointed one would live in man and man would live in Him. Note also that hope is a part of the mystery; *"hope"* is **the joyful expectation to be glorified with Christ at His return.**

Colossians 1:28
> **Whom we preach, warning every man, and teaching every man in all wisdom; that we may present every man perfect in Christ Jesus:**

It is my responsibility to preach the revelation of the mystery, to warn those who might reject the gospel and to teach the wisdom of God that makes one perfect in Christ.

<u>In this I labor according to the working of the mystery in me, to fulfill the Word of God</u>. This is the mandate of every apostle; the Word of God must **first** be fulfilled in us. We must be the living proof of what we preach and teach. It is only then that we will be able to establish others in the mystery of Christ. Some in the Body of Christ are not fully established in Him and the main reason for this has been that the basics of their belief or faith have been taught from an erroneous perspective.

"Perspective" is the place from which boundaries originate. **Perspective proceeds from God's eternal purpose.** It is from His purpose that the worlds were formed. He created man, He installed the law; and He sent the Word to planet Earth in the form of flesh. **<u>God's perspective comes from His heart and mind and has created the boundaries in which the Sons of God are to relate to Him and their fellow man.</u>**

If the foundation of our theological perspective is off, it leaves even the Bible scholars open to error. Very often pastors preach from perspectives that have been handed down and do not realize the error. They have not rightly divided the scriptures for themselves, or may not even know how to do so.

When the Lord visited me in 1985, He sent me to the Church to deliver a pure and sure Word that would bring forth His purpose in the lives of His people. This is the Word and the work He gave me to do. Since then I have been at times discouraged having seen how Satan has successfully infiltrated the Church with the doctrines of devils. These doctrines have all but totally destroyed the way of the common salvation of old. Satan has taken a seat in the Church and has been made quite comfortable. Well, he can afford to be comfortable, as the saints of God are working diligently to accomplish the things outlined in his doctrines.

PERSPECTIVE

1. The realm in which a doctrine sits
Jesus Christ is the author and finisher of our faith. It is His mind that sets the boundaries for what we are to believe, think, feel and do. It is the mind of Christ that sets the "boundaries of the faith."

2. To see as God sees
Jesus declared, "I do only those things I see the Father do. My words are not my own, they are the Father's." The Word of God was made flesh in Jesus Christ. It sets the boundaries for what Christ did, thought, felt and believed. He remained obedient to the will of the Father.

3. Always produces the purpose of God
Only the correct perspective of truth will produce the purity of the gospel and only the purity of the Word will produce a true Son of God. Consider the following:

A >>The Son must not accept any word that is not the mind of Christ>> B

Babe   **Maturity**

The backdrop and staging for all doctrines of the Bible is the mind of Christ. All scripture was fulfilled in Him. His is the life that has been tried and tested before the Father; His is the life the Father has accepted. He is the prototype for all the Sons who will follow.

Chapter Eight
FAITH IS NOT . . .

In order for me or any other theologian to teach faith effectively, we must first convince you of God's perspective. I sincerely hope that the previous chapter accomplished that. However, I feel led to keep this perspective in view as we proceed. **Remember, Christianity is not a lifestyle; it is a "life." It is literally the "life of Jesus Christ" being lived out in earthen vessels.**

Beloved, you cannot dissect Christ. You must accept all of Him or none. When we walk after the Spirit we walk in the mind of Christ. Again I say to you, "It is impossible to walk in the mind of Christ and not take on His <u>emotions</u>, <u>desires</u>, <u>attributes</u> and <u>character</u>. It is also impossible not to walk in His faith." *For the life we live now in the flesh, we live by the faith of Jesus Christ (Gal. 2:20).* This is the reality of the Sons. His faith has been tried and tested and found to be lacking nothing.

We need to stop and consider that the scripture does intend for us to be as Christ was in this world today. That includes the fact that Christ was not running around yelling "money cometh." Neither did He ever stand on a platform and zap His congregation into material prosperity. Furthermore, we cannot find any messages where His central theme or subject matter was "how to obtain the wealth of this world." Jesus was concerned about souls and ministry. [He never set a man on a path that uses faith to acquire the things of this world.] To the contrary His message was, *Love not the world nor the things of the world, for all that is in the world is the lust of the flesh, the lust of the eye and the pride of life (I John 2:15-16).*

What do we do with Jesus' comment about the rich young ruler, whom He told to go and sell all that he had and then come and follow Him? As the man dropped his head in sadness, Jesus replied that it was easier for a camel to go through the eye of a needle than it was for a rich man to enter the kingdom. If this was the case then why would Jesus and the Father insist on giving us the wealth of this world in this present time, knowing that it is likely to pull us away from Him?

Paul wrote to Timothy warning him of the mindset of many men of God who had corrupted themselves and the people they led. But some diehards in an attempt to hold on to the faith and prosperity connection try to place the focus of the passages below on unbelievers or the unsaved. However, the 10th verse settles that issue. *For the love of money is the root of all evil: which while some coveted after, **they have erred from the faith**, and pierced themselves through with many sorrows.* In order for one to err from the faith, one must first be in the faith. So I want you to read these scriptures very carefully, as they express the disposition of much of the leadership and their following in the Body today.

I Timothy 6:5-11
5 Perverse disputings of men of corrupt minds, and destitute of the truth, <u>supposing that gain is godliness:</u> from such withdraw thyself. Listen to the preacher as he goes directly to the bottom line. He implies that those who teach such doctrines are corrupt in their minds; therefore they do not walk in the mind of Christ. They are also destitute or void of the truth. Yes, there are a lot of truths within some of

their teachings, but as I stated in an earlier chapter, when truth is ministered from an improper perspective the result can only be a perverted gospel.

Paul goes on to say these men suppose or assume that material gain is evidence of God's glory in our lives. If such is the case, then what is the evidence of His glory in the lives of those who came into the Body with great wealth; those whose profession or worldly affairs caused them to acquire much material gain before they even met Christ? As Paul stated, this is indeed an assumption. It has no scriptural basis for the New Testament Church.

Now the instructions are clear; *"From such withdraw yourself."* It is amazing how the preacher can tell us not to bid an individual Godspeed if he should come preaching any other doctrine other than that of the apostles' doctrine. Still many are willing to turn away from every false teaching except that of earthly prosperity. I sincerely hope that will not be the case after you have finished this study.

6 But godliness with contentment is great gain. The world is not enjoying contentment and neither is the Church. It is not the order of the day. To be content with what God has given is almost considered a slanderous thing against God.

I know that by now some of you are thinking, "Well, I know where she's going with this. This is another one of those poverty advocates." Although the scriptures do declare we will have the poor among us always, and not to mention how Paul did go about collecting monies from some of the churches to help the poor saints at Jerusalem, *(Rom 15:26)*. This is not a poverty doctrine. It is a doctrine that says all things were created by Him and for Him.

Those who walk after the Spirit will be able to gain access to much material wealth to be used in the establishing of the covenant. They will use it to finance the Gospel of the Kingdom but it is the Father however who will channel the finances to meet the needs and the overall scope of the ministry. He will never renew the vanity of the flesh. I use the term "access" because many of us will not physically own the resources needed to further this message, but the Father is committed to leading, guiding and putting us in the paths of those who are ready and willing to help get this Word to the masses.

My ministry is one such ministry. I believe we have learned and lived enough in this way for the Lord to be able to trust us with the finances needed to get this Word out. But to this date we would be considered a very financially poor ministry. We do not have the big bucks, the great cathedrals or the mega donor base. However, I am not careful concerning this matter. It is time for this Word to come to the Body and the Lord has assured me that He has prepared hearts that are willing and able to finance His truth. There are those who will see it as the greatest investment of their lives.

7 For we brought nothing into this world, and it is certain we can carry nothing out. I don't think it gets any plainer than this. Paul is trying desperately to destroy an erroneous mindset about materialism in this world. It is not the intent of the Father for us to be in hot pursuit of things.

8 And having food and raiment let us be therewith content. One thing can truly be said of the writers of the New Testament; their teachings were extremely consistent with those of Christ Jesus.

In Luke 12:22, Jesus said to His disciples; ". . . *Therefore I say unto you, Take no thought for your life, what ye shall eat; neither for the body, what ye shall put on."* This must be the mind of those who will please the Father. If not, lust and the spirit of the world will be allowed once again to rule and reign in their life.

If those who desire to be rich are subject to fall into foolish and hurtful lusts that drown men in destruction, why would the wealth of this world be the focal point of any message in the Church? The Lord knows how to finance that which is His. He does not need to defame His glory by pointing men and women to the world for personal gain. Once again I quote the 9th verse of this chapter; *But they that will be rich fall into temptation and a snare, and into many foolish and hurtful lusts which drown men in destruction and perdition.*

The Father shows that the end result of the acquisition of personal wealth is to give us pre-eminence, power and authority in the lives of others. He knows many will not be able to handle personal gain, but will indeed become victims of lusts that lead to destruction. This is truly the mind of the Father. It is plain and simple. This message is literal and needs no philosophical interpretation.

We have established then that this warning and commandment is written to the people of God (those in the Faith). To covet the riches of this world is error and to make material wealth synonymous with the glory of God in the New Testament Church is "heresy".

11 But thou, O man of God, flee these things; and follow after righteousness, godliness, faith, love, patience,

meekness.   As the songwriter said, "Run and don't look back, you better run."   Depart from this doctrine that keeps you in hot pursuit of the things of the world, promising you great wealth that can only be seen in houses, land, cars, jewels and clothes.   How cheap the blood of Jesus has become!   Do you believe that He was humiliated and crucified just so that we would have the same things that others got by profession or just plain hard work?

I love to shop. What woman doesn't? I also like nice things. But I am instructed; in whatsoever state I am, therewith to be content.   Therefore, I know both how to be abased, and I know how to abound: everywhere and in all things I am instructed both to be full and to be hungry, both to abound and to suffer need *(Phil 4:11-12).*

Bear with me a moment while I stir up your pure mind to think on those things that are contrary to the mind of Christ and the preaching of the apostles. If you understood the previous chapters, then you didn't miss the fact that we are spiritual beings. We are the Sons of the Most High; His children, His offspring. We are divine in nature, circumcised in the flesh. The promises of our Father, (who is the Father of spirits, Heb. 12:9), are spiritual blessings. They include the supernatural power of God to be a witness of the truth and to work ministry in the lives of His people.

No, my brothers and sisters in the Lord, faith is not for the acquisition of things. Now that we have discussed what it is not, let us go on to discuss what faith for the Sons of God really is.

Chapter Nine
FAITH IS . . .

I can hear the Holy Ghost even now saying, "Go directly to the heart of the matter and explain the true meaning of faith." I must obey. Afterwards, we will work our way back to pick up all the supporting details in the script. All I ask of you is that you maintain an open heart and mind. This does not mean that you cannot challenge this lesson, but do so inside of the Holy Canon. Let the scriptures be our final authority. I must caution you also not to jump the gun. If I say something that you just do not agree with, that is fair. Nevertheless, please continue the study and hear the conclusion of the matter.

GOD'S DEFINITION OF FAITH

When the Lord visited me in this revelation, He took me to the most quoted, but often most misunderstood verse of scripture relating to faith. Keep in mind that the mystery of God is hidden inside of simplicity.

Hebrews 11:1
> *Now faith is the substance of things hoped*
> *for, And the evidence of things not seen.*

A. Faith is the substance:

Strong's Concordance defines the Greek *Huparxis* and *Hupostasis... "substance"* as to be in existence, possession, **the real nature of that to which reference is made in contrast to the outward manifestation. It speaks of the**

divine essence of God, existent and expressed in the revelation of His Son.

Webster's dictionary defines the word **"*substance*"** as: **The essence of a thing, that which makes it real, or the essential part of something**. For example: Adam was formed from the dust of the earth, however, that body could not function until the essential part (the breath of life or wind) was put into it. One can lose an arm or even lose both arms and continue to live; however, when you take the breath or the essential part away, there is no life.

Note also that we are now the Sons of God. We were created in the image of Jesus Christ. Therefore, substance for us is also the divine essence of God, existent and expressed in the revelation of our adoption into the royal family.

Remember, the mysteries of the Word are found in its simplicity. Follow the simplicity of the script here.

Hebrews 11:1 Faith is the substance of things hoped for.... or it is the essential part or true nature of the things hoped for. That essential part is the divine essence or nature of God, existent and expressed. Therefore, <u>Faith is the essential part or true nature of the things we hope for but have not seen</u>.

B. Things that are hoped for but not seen:

Exactly what are the things we were hoping for? This is very important, because this is where the trail splits. The "Faith and Prosperity" message placed the **Church** in hope of acquiring the wealth of this world. Therefore, the church began to lay claim to the blessings God promised the nation of Israel in Deuteronomy, Chapters 28 and 29.

Deuteronomy 28:2

> *And all these blessings shall come upon thee and over take thee, if thou shall hearken unto the voice of the Lord thy God.*

These famous faith chapters were the blessings that the law provided for Israel and were all natural or earthy in content. Everything that was promised under the law could be found in this world. Israel would be a naturally blessed nation of people if they continued to abide in the laws of God.

- He would indeed make them the head and not the tail in this world.
- He would bless them in the fields and in the storehouses.
- He would bless them going in and coming out.
- The ground that they tread upon would indeed be an everlasting possession.

However, the nation of Israel did not adhere to the laws of the first covenant. Therefore, we see the installation of a new and better covenant.

Hebrews 8:7-9, 13

> *7 For if that first covenant had been faultless, then should no place have been sought for the second,*
> *8 For finding fault with them, he saith, Behold, the days come, saith the Lord, when I will make*

a new covenant with the house of Israel and with the house of Judah:

9 Not according to the covenant that I made with their fathers in the day when I took them by the hand to lead them out of the land of Egypt; because they continued not in my covenant, and I regarded them not, saith the Lord . . .

13 In that he saith, A new covenant, he hath made the first old. Now that which decayeth and waxeth old is ready to vanish away.

It is not expedient for the clergy to assign the attributes of the Old Covenant to the New Testament Church. This has spelled tragedy for the Body of Christ. The Father is very clear in His intent and purposes here. He sent His Son to be the testator of a new covenant.

Hebrews 8:6

*But now hath he obtained a more excellent ministry, by how much also he is the mediator of <u>**a better covenant**</u>, which was established upon <u>**better promises**</u>.*

My dear brethren you cannot get around this truth. If you insist on teaching the materialistic blessings of the Old Covenant to the New Testament Church, then you must simply ignore the truth that is laid out here in these and other passages.

The things we are to hope for are the things the Lord has promised us as a **Church**. <u>Even so, in order for Israel to be a partaker of the promises of the second covenant, they too, must accept the work of the mediator of the second covenant.</u> ***Blessed be the God and Father of our Lord Jesus Christ,*** *who hath blessed us with all spiritual blessings in heavenly places in Christ (Ephesians 1:3).*

Here we find the key that unlocks the mystery. The Father promised the **Church** spiritual blessings. This follows logic, considering we are a **spiritual race**. We are the Sons of God, members of the divine family and the royal priesthood. We are not as natural Israel, neither were we given the same promises. The Lord has established Himself a Church, a body of baptized believers in Christ, which includes both the Jew, and the Gentile. The following scriptures highlight the things that the Body of Christ has been promised but have not seen yet hope for.

St. John 3:16

> *For God so loved the world that he gave his only begotten Son, that whosoever believeth in him should not perish but have everlasting life.*

I John 5:11

> *And this is the record, that God has given to us eternal life, and this life is in his Son.*

Here, we see one of the promises made to the **Church** was that of **eternal life**. Those who became partakers of the new birth would live forever. This far exceeds any natural reward. **This is a spiritual blessing for a spiritual people.** Nevertheless, we have not seen the saints of God live forever. Instead saints continue to die every day and are buried in our graveyards. No, we have not yet seen the manifestation of this promise but we indeed hope for it. It is our blessed hope that should we die in this world we shall live again in the next.

I Corinthians 15:51-53

51   Behold, I shew you a mystery; We shall not all sleep, but we shall all be changed,

52   In a moment, in the twinkling of an eye, at the last trump: for the trumpet shall sound, and the dead shall be raised incorruptible, and we shall be changed.

*53   **For this corruptible must put on incorruption, and this mortal must put on immortality.***

Note verse 53: ***For this corruption must put on incorruption, and this mortal must put on immortality.*** This is yet another promise from the Father. We are promised a glorious **new body**. Paul reiterates this point even further to the churches throughout Asia.

II Corinthians 5:1-7

*1 For we know that if our earthly house of this tabernacle were dissolved, **we have a building of God, an house not made with hands, eternal in the heavens.***

*2 For in this we groan, earnestly desiring to be **clothed upon with our house which is from heaven:***

3 If so be that being clothed we shall not be found naked.

4 For we that are in this tabernacle do groan, being burdened: not for that we would be unclothed, but clothed upon, that mortality might be swallowed up of life.

5 Now he that hath wrought us for the selfsame thing is God, who also hath given unto us the earnest of the Spirit.
6 Therefore we are always confident, knowing that, whilst we are at home in the body, we are absent from the Lord:
 *7 **(For we walk by faith, not by sight:)***

Note also Paul admits that the church had not as yet seen such a thing manifested. However, he declares, "we walk by faith, not by sight." Although we have not seen it, yet we do hope for it.

Romans 8:18-21

*18 **For I reckon that the sufferings of this present time are not worthy to be compared with the glory which shall be revealed in us.***
*19 **For the earnest expectation of the creature waiteth for the manifestation of the sons of God.***
*20 **For the creature was made subject to vanity, not willingly, but by reason of him who hath subjected the same in hope,***
*21 **Because the creature itself also shall be delivered from the bondage of corruption into the glorious liberty of the children of God.***

The creature (the new man, the regenerated spiritual being) is waiting for the time of the revealing of the Sons of God. He is moaning, groaning, and travailing to be delivered from this body of vanity. He is the Son of God **awaiting his new body.** Though he was made subject or caused to remain in the body, he was also subjected to hope. Yes, the hope of being delivered into the glorious liberty of the Sons of God.

For we are saved by hope: but hope that is seen is not hope: for what a man seeth, why doth he yet hope for? But if we hope for that we see not, then do we with patience wait for it (Romans 8: 24-25).

We have not seen our new bodies, but we do with patience wait for them. For we know that each of us has a new tabernacle, not made with hands, eternal in the heavens, waiting for us. Therefore, the things hoped for and things unseen are:

1. **ETERNAL LIFE**
2. **THE NEW BODY**

C. Faith is the evidence...

The word *"evidence"* is defined as: ***proof, or a witness***. Why is our hope so strong? Well, the answer is simple. The one who has wrought this thing in us is God, who has also given unto us the earnest of the Spirit *(I Cor. 5:5)*. **God has given unto us the Holy Ghost. He has given us the earnest, essential part or substance of the new body.** Beloved, this is so powerful! He has given us the witness on the inside. His very Spirit now testifies of the power of our God. Therefore, as Paul said, we are confident. We not only believe, we have the evidence of His faithfulness. Furthermore, we do not walk as others, but we walk by the hope given to us by the Spirit of God.

Romans 8:15-16

> *15   For ye have not received the spirit of bondage again to fear; but ye have received the Spirit of adoption, whereby we cry, Abba, Father.*

***16   The Spirit itself beareth witness with our
spirit, that we are the children of God:***

We have received the Spirit of adoption and are now the children of God.   What is the evidence of such a great blessing? The 16th verse makes it quite clear. "The Spirit itself bears witness with our spirit, that we are the children of God." Now because we are the children of God, we are then His heirs, and this also makes us joint heirs with Christ Jesus.

Beloved, this is the only evidence you have in proclaiming yourself to be a Son of God.   Likewise, it is the only evidence that you have inherited eternal life.   The Holy Ghost, the Spirit of the Living God, is your only proof of such truths. He, the Holy Spirit, is the witness! He is the Comforter, the one sent to bear witness of the Lordship of Jesus Christ.

Ask yourself, "What other proof or evidence do you have of eternal life? How do you know that you are saved? What other witness do you have other than the Holy Ghost?" He is the evidence of the things you hope for but have not seen.

Romans 8:20, 24-25
>*20   For the creature was made subject to vanity, not willingly, but by reason of him who hath subjected the same in hope…*
>*24   **For we are saved by hope: but hope that is seen is not hope: for what a man seeth, why doth he yet hope for***?
>*25   But if we hope for that we see not, then do we with patience wait for it.*

It is essential that you agree with the Lord right here. Faith is for things that are hoped for and the things we hope for are the things that we have not seen. *For we walk by faith, not by sight.* My brethren, please be careful not to spiritualize this issue. Faith is for the asking and receiving of things that are unseen. It is spiritual in both its nature and its workings. I beg you not to continue in a vein that reduces the work of the cross to the acquisition of things. In many circles it does not take a lot of faith to get a car, or a house, or large bank account. As my physician said to me, "Mary if faith is about cars, houses, land and money, I already have those things. My profession gave me the finer things in this life. What is the message the **Church** offers me and others like me?"

The Father subjected the new creature to hope. Hope is not waiting in uncertainty, which is the connotation some place on it. **But hope means to wait with joy and patience for the promise of the Father, knowing that it is a sure Word.** The new creature is to live in this body that is one day going back to the dust, but in the meanwhile he is to wait with a joyful expectation of his new body and eternal life with the Father and the Son.

Let us continue to stay with the simplicity of the script.

Faith is . . .

I.   The Substance (the essential part) of things hoped for

    A.   New Body
    B.   Eternal Life

II. The Evidence (proof or witness) of things not seen:

A. **New Body**
B. **Eternal Life**

FAITH IS the substance or essential part of eternal life. It is also the evidence or proof we have a new body not made with hands, waiting for us in heaven. God has dealt to every man (Son) the measure of faith.

The essential part of eternal life and the new body is the Holy Ghost and the only evidence or witness of the existence of eternal life and the new body is the Holy Ghost. Furthermore, the only thing God has dealt to every one of us is His Spirit.   Beloved, for the Sons of God; **FAITH IS THE HOLY GHOST.**

I want so very much for you to understand this lesson because the very essence of your spiritual growth depends on it. When the Lord ministered this to me my whole perspective of the Word of God changed. Immediately the stress was taken out of ministry. I didn't have to psych myself up to believe anything. All I had to do was believe in the Christ within me. It was His faith that was doing the work and living the life in this body. <u>I simply had to agree with Him and not seek my own routes or ways</u>.

If you are to comprehend the things of God, you will need to understand that **Faith is a dispensation. It is the method by which God is dealing with His people in this age.**

Paul told the church at Galatia, *"But before faith came, we were kept under the law, shut up unto the faith which should afterwards be revealed," Gal 3:23.* This means that Faith goes beyond our ability to believe God. You may say, "How so, Mary?" Well, the old patriots believed the spoken Word of God, but they did not live in the dispensation of faith. *"But the scripture hath concluded all under sin, that the promise by faith of Jesus Christ might be given to them that believe, Gal 3:22.* Faith for this dispensation is that which is given to us by the Father. He knew that our human faith just might not be sufficient for the trials ahead. Thus, before Christ suffered His passion, knowing the effect it would have on Peter and the other disciples, He spoke to him. *But I have prayed for thee, that thy faith fail not: and when thou art converted, strengthen thy brethren (St. Luke 22:32).*

I am sure you can identify with this trend of thought. When we do not walk after the Spirit, there are days in which circumstances, situations and relationships cause us to doubt or waver in our belief and trust. But if in fact, walking in and after the Spirit places our walk back inside the life of Christ, then it also follows that the life we live now, we live by the **faith of Jesus Christ.**

The scriptures below reveal and project the fact that Jesus is the author and finisher of our faith. It began with Him and it will end with Him.

*Galatians 3:23 "But **before faith came**, we were kept under the law, shut up unto the faith which should afterwards be revealed."* We are discussing a faith that came and was revealed after the Law.

*Galatians 2:16 "Knowing that a man is not justified by the works of the law, but by **the faith of Jesus Christ**, even we have believed in Jesus Christ, **that we might be justified by the faith of Christ**, and not by the works of the law: for by* the works of the law shall no flesh be justified." Listen to Paul carefully here. We have believed in Jesus Christ so that we can be justified by His faith. We have received the promise the patriots waited for and died believing in. It was the promise of the faith of Jesus Christ that justifies and perfects. And these all, having obtained a good report through faith, (their belief in the coming Christ), received not the promise: God having provided some better thing for us, that they (the Old Covenant saints), without us should not be made perfect *(Heb 11:39-40)*. Perfection came with the faith of Christ. **Faith is the walk in the Holy Ghost, which is the Spirit of Christ that makes us perfect before God.**

Galatians 3:22 *"But the scripture hath concluded all under sin, that the promise by faith of Jesus Christ might be given to them that believe."* We have already discovered that the promise is the Spirit. Here, Paul makes the promise (the Spirit) equal to, or synonymous with faith. This faith is given to those who believe. Once again, we are encouraged to believe on Jesus Christ. The life we live in the flesh is His life.

Romans 3:22 *"Even the righteousness of God which is by faith of Jesus Christ unto all and upon all them that believe: for there is no difference:".* The righteousness of God can only be obtained by walking in the faith of Jesus Christ. This righteousness and faith is again given to those who believe.

Revelation 14:12 *"Here is the patience of the saints: here are they that keep the commandments of God, and the faith of Jesus".* At the end of the mystery, the reward of glory will be bestowed upon those who keep, or hold fast to, the faith of Jesus Christ.

Yes, there are some passages of script where Webster's definition of faith as mere trust and belief do apply, but the deeper meaning of the term is found in God's purpose for the **Church**. If you dare give yourself a little more time and consider that the Lord may be able to open the eyes of your understanding through these lessons, then bear with me. You have nothing to lose, except the frustration of not knowing some of the deeper things of God.

Faith is spiritual and it is for a spiritual people to do a spiritual work. It is the mechanism by which we are to work ministry.

I Corinthians 12:4,7
> *4 Now there are diversities of gifts, but the same Spirit.*
> *7 But the manifestation of the Spirit is given to every man to profit withal.*

In the next lessons I will go into much more detail concerning this matter of Faith. You will begin to understand that Faith (the Holy Ghost) is not dependent upon whether or not you believe for the favorable outcome of a situation. It is more dependent upon whether you believe in and agree with the Christ within you as He lives and moves throughout that situation. You will also understand that faith is purely an operation of God. I love the Body of Christ, and I am so concerned that it receives the truth in this due season.

Chapter Ten
OPPOSING YOUR FAITH

God's plan for man included sending His Word to dwell in human flesh for thirty-three and a half years. Jesus Christ became the first begotten of the Father and His ministry lasted three and a half years. His mission was that of reconciliation, as God was in Christ reconciling the world unto Himself.

Jesus promised to send those who believed on Him a Comforter, after He returned to the Father. This Comforter we know to be the Holy Ghost. He is the Spirit of God, the Life of Christ, and the substance of our faith. Nevertheless, it is the life of Christ that I want you to see. You must understand that the life of Jesus Christ lives in you. That life is the same today as it was 2000 years ago.

Romans 12:3

> *For I say, through the grace given unto me, to every man that is among you, not to think of himself more highly than he ought to think; but to think soberly, according as <u>God hath dealt to every man the measure of faith</u>.*

The scripture declares that God has dealt to every one of us the measure of Faith. We must consider that the only thing we have received from God is the Holy Ghost. Everything He has dispensed is in the Spirit He has given us. It follows therefore, that the faith He gave us is in the Holy Ghost. The Holy Ghost being the life of Jesus is His faith that we have received. This is important because it takes the stress out of trying to walk in faith. All we have to do is obey the Christ within, and walk in His Spirit. His faith has already been tried and tested and has never failed.

While Christ was here on earth everything that He did or said was in accordance to, reliant on, and of complete trust in what the Father had said. His life was completely sold out to doing the will of the Father. There was never an issue with Him as to whether or not He was going to obey God. The Bible says Christ was obedient unto death, even the death of the cross. He knew that His life was in God's hands. He knew that His body would not see corruption (decay) and that He would be raised from the dead. He believed it because God said it. He knew that the Father was faithful and could not lie. This same Faith (adhering to, relying on, and completely trusting God) is in each and every one of us who have accepted Christ. This faith is part of our inheritance in Christ.

Let me spell out right here your responsibility in this equation. You must supply faith in the Christ that is in you. You must believe on Him the way the scripture has said *(St. John 7:38)*. The Father does not expect this to be hard, considering you have already experienced the power of Christ. Your faith in Him is manifested in your obedience. To obey is to walk in the Spirit of Christ. Accepting this premise, we must look into that which hinders the church from walking in that faith.

Galatians 2:20

> *I am crucified with Christ: nevertheless I live; yet not I, but Christ liveth in me: and the life which I now live in the flesh I live by the faith of the Son of God, who loved me, and gave himself for me.*

This scripture forces you to examine the true operation of your salvation. The old man of sin is dead He is crucified with Christ. The source of life for your body now is the Spirit of Christ Jesus, (the Holy Ghost). Because the old man of sin died in Christ, it is lawful for him to be raised in Christ. These are the facts and this is the good news, the report that was not believed. **We, the Sons of God live by the power of the indwelling Christ;** He is our source of life. The Father has not given us the spirit of the world again to fear but that of Jesus Christ, the conqueror of death. In Him we live, walk, and overcome the temptations of this world.

Philippians 2:5

> *Let this mind be in you, which was also in Christ Jesus:*

According to the above passage, it is your responsibility to allow the mind of Christ to be in you. It follows therefore that you can deny that mind. You have the ability to refuse to be led by the Spirit; you can choose your own path. The bottom line is . . . you can refuse to obey God. Christ also had the same choice. In making your decision though, consider this:

I John 1:5-7

> *5 This then is the message which we have heard of him, and declare unto you, that God is light, and <u>in him is no darkness at all</u>.*
> *6 If we say that we have fellowship with him, and walk in darkness, we lie, and do not the truth:*
> *7 But if we walk in the light, as he is in the light, we have fellowship one with another, and*

the blood of Jesus Christ his Son cleanseth us from all sin.

If you choose not to walk in the life of Christ, then you choose to walk in darkness and death. As I stated earlier, Christ is the same today as He was yesterday and the scriptures clearly define our relationship to Him.

I John 4:17

Herein is our love made perfect, that we may have boldness in the day of judgment: because as he is, so are we in this world.

To walk in the Spirit is to be as Christ is. He came to reconcile men to God and now we have been given the ministry of reconciliation. To walk in the Spirit allows us to experience the same passion for our brothers in the world as Christ has. Furthermore, His Spirit being the source of our lives, genders Godly character and emotions.

Christ is continuing His mission in our bodies. He remains focused on the will of the Father, willing to obey at any cost. This is the mind of Christ today as He lives in you. You must take on or allow this mind to operate by not quenching or grieving the Holy Ghost. Obedience to the mind of Christ is your salvation; to do otherwise is death, hell and destruction.

WALLS OF IMPASSE

Let us continue to investigate why the Faith of Christ has not been consistent in our lives.

A. WANTONNESS: Unlawful desires, lust and consideration of self; sin. One of the major oppositions in the Body of Christ, generally, has been wantonness. *"Wantonness"* is **desires or even mindsets for which you are willing to break the laws of God to fulfill.** Wantonness has kept men from walking in the power, authority and faith of Christ. It has been a crippler in the Church.

It is in the hearts of men that desires, emotions, affections and appetites exist. Your strong desires and mindsets have persisted in your heart because you have protected and shielded them from the influence of the Word of God. Pride is the mechanism used to shield the areas of the heart that house your most protected wants and private beliefs.

James 5:5

> *Ye have lived in pleasure on the earth, and been wanton; ye have nourished your hearts, as in a day of slaughter.*

As a result of wantonness the world will not see the Sons functioning and operating in the totality of faith, (the operation of the Holy Ghost). It will only see those who have a form of godliness, but who deny the power thereof. Jesus prayed for the Father to make us one with them and each other, but want, greed and lust forbid this. So the question before you today is, "What is it that you want so much that you are not willing to do without it? What is it that is hindering the life of Christ from being manifested? Could it be sex, a car, a house, a job, or money? Or, could it just be your way of thinking?" Whatever that thing is, it must be eradicated from your being. Be honest with God and yourself; you know the answers to these questions. You are not in the dark concerning the desires that hold your mind captive. Remember, the truth shall make you free.

B. INIQUITY: Lawlessness, that which stops the flow of love. Another reason the faith of Christ has not been consistent in the lives of the Sons of God is iniquity. When it comes to obeying the Word, the Sons have been lawless.

The source of much of the iniquity in the Body of Christ is offenses. When offenses linger there is rarely an application of the Word, as such an application would force the continued flow of love and unity. Once the Word is rejected, offenses reign. It becomes more appealing to retaliate, or just give the offender a piece of your mind. In some instances you may have withheld your affections as a means of punishing your offender. The Word of God is constantly set aside time after time. To forgive and to recompense no man evil for evil, but to overcome evil with good have been mere quotations. The focus has shifted from pleasing the Father. High-mindedness and retribution are now the order of the day.

1. HIGH-MINDEDNESS

Many in the Body have thought too much of themselves. They are standing on pedestals demanding submission, obedience and in some cases worship.

II Corinthians 10:3-5

> *3 For though we walk in the flesh, we do not war after the flesh:*
> *4(For the weapons of our warfare are not carnal, but mighty through God to the pulling down of strong holds;)*

5 Casting down imaginations, and every high thing that exalteth itself against the knowledge of God, and bringing into captivity every thought to the obedience of Christ;

Authority has been given to the leadership in your life to cast down every high thing that exalts itself above the knowledge of God. It is my responsibility to tell you the truth. Sometimes that truth may seem cruel and cold, but then sin of any kind is cruel and cold. Examine yourself to see if you are in the faith. You know the drill. Document the place where you stand in the Word: what is the nature of your fruit? What is the image you have of yourself? If it is not the image of Christ, then it needs to be destroyed.

2. RETRIBUTION: payback; a passion for emotional or physical satisfaction, vengeance

Love never needs to be avenged; it has no enemies. Instead, it bears the infirmities of others. It is hard for some to allow themselves to forgive without a penalty. Men especially see this as a sign of weakness. If you allow your ego to get in the way, when will you ever turn the other cheek?

I Peter 2:21-23

21 For even hereunto were ye called: because Christ also suffered for us, leaving us an example, that ye should follow his steps:
22 Who did no sin, neither was guile found in his mouth:
23 Who, when he was reviled, reviled not again; when he suffered, he threatened not; but committed himself to him that judgeth righteously:

Walking after the flesh brings no pleasure to God. We must do that which is acceptable unto Him. However, in order to do so you must walk in the Faith of Christ. Remember, it is not about the other person, or the situation itself, but it is about your submission to God.

3. PRIDE: Self-exaltation and an unnatural love for one's self.

Another wall of impasse has been pride. Pride is self-exaltation. Given any relationship, whether friendship, marriage or blood relations, if there is any contention, then pride is manifest.

Proverb 13:10

>*Only by pride cometh contention: but with the well advised is wisdom.*

We should be able to disagree without becoming contentious. God hates pride (*Proverbs 8:13*), **Pride goeth before destruction and an haughty spirit before a fall** (*Proverb 16:18*). Pride and wantonness go hand in hand. Pride will keep you in lust and wantonness. We learned many years ago that pride is not a friend.

4. REBELLION AND STUBBORNNESS. We have seen over the years how rebellion and stubbornness can wreak havoc in a home, church or community.

The major attributes of rebellion are:
- Going against or opposing that which you have been a part of;
- Going against established order;

- Rejecting of known truth.

There have been many situations in ministry where rebellion has been prevalent. It has manifested itself through offenses, wantonness and a lust for ministry. Many leave their churches to live out the lusts of their heart or mind.

Rebellion and stubbornness can also manifest themselves in those who sit in church week after week, singing in the choir or working on the deacon board or some other activity in the household of Faith. These individuals either directly or indirectly oppose established authority. They do not respect the government of God, nor do they regard the casualties that result from their disrespect of God's people or His Word. **If you walk in rebellion or stubbornness then the only thing that matters is what you want at that time.** No amount of truth can persuade you. In fact, truth becomes an offense. Until you begin to see rebellion and stubbornness the way God sees it, you will continue to walk in it.

I Samuel 15:23

> *For rebellion is as the sin of witchcraft, and stubbornness is as iniquity and idolatry. Because thou hast rejected the word of the LORD, he hath also rejected thee from being king.*

The Lord puts rebellion in the same category as witchcraft. He places stubbornness in the same category as idolatry. This is a serious matter. Look at the latter part of I Samuel 15:23, *"Because thou hast rejected the word of the LORD, he hath also rejected thee from being king."* **IF YOU REJECT GOD OR HIS WORD, HE WILL REJECT YOU.**

Men so often do not see their actions as rebellious. But even as God sent instructions to Saul by Samuel (the prophet) He also instructs us through our leaders. As with Saul, the Sons of God today still decide what they will and will not obey of the Lord. As long as it is something that is pleasing to the flesh or something you can agree with or understand you may follow instructions to the letter. However, if God's instructions become unpleasant to the flesh or you do not agree with or understand them, then pride will dictate your response. Remember, a lack of understanding is no justification for pride. Meekness will always open the door for understanding. Saul simply chose not to obey and God rejected him. Your rebellion says to God, "I am an idol worshipper and the image I worship is me."

Stubbornness can be very costly. It can rob you of peace and contentment. A man can know for example that his wife is the better person to handle the finances, but because he is a male and his father may have said, *"You must control your house,"* that man will never allow his wife to do those things that she does best in the management of the home. His stubbornness becomes more important than having a sound financial statement.

One of the major attributes of faith is spiritual alienation from the world. (We are in the world, but not of this world). When your character and personality interfere with the life of Christ, lust and wantonness for the things of this world become a driving force. The lust of the mind stimulates your members and creates desire for the things of this world. You are the offspring of God. Therefore, it is no longer the devil or some demonic spirit living within you creating this lust. It is your own thinking. You, too, are perfect until the day the iniquity **you** created is found in your heart. That is why you must be steadfast in renewing your mind. You must allow (let) this mind that was in Christ Jesus be in you. Every aspect of your life should be according to the faith of Christ.

Jesus did not attach Himself to things on planet Earth, but He set His affections on things above. **He was a pilgrim passing through. He knew His purpose was to do the will of the Father**. If Christ is to live through us, then we too must live as pilgrims, just passing through this world.

Hebrews 10:38

> *Now the just shall live by faith: but if any man draw back, my soul shall have no pleasure in him.*

Let us not draw back but let us go on and live by the Faith of Christ. You can do it. It will bring perfect peace in your life.

Chapter Eleven
FAITH IN ADVERSITY

The devil has created false doctrines and introduced foreign mindsets to the people of God in an attempt to hinder the spiritual development of the Sons of God. There are those of us, however, who are not moved by the sleight of men or Satan himself. We know in whom we have believed. Nevertheless, we all must come to that place of maturity that begs for the opportunity to glorify the Father. Believe it or not, it is easy to walk in the power of our Christ.

Romans 8:14

> *For as many as are led by the Spirit of God, they are the sons of God.*

This scripture sets the boundaries and establishes the criteria for those whom God considers to be His Sons. It also takes us beyond the indwelling of the Holy Ghost for eternal security. It implies that you must supply a walk, led by the Spirit of God. You must also be willing to remain in fellowship with the Father for His guidance through adverse situations. We must believe that God is in total control of our life and that the Spirit of Faith orchestrates those things we deal with from day to day.

St. John 19:11

> *Jesus answered, Thou couldest have no power at all against me, except it were given thee from above: therefore he that delivered me unto thee hath the greater sin.*

Here we see Jesus **believed** and **accepted** the fact that the Spirit of God directed and ordered those situations that were unfavorable to His flesh. Here is where most saints would not dare or even think to go. God will lead you into adversity and persecution at the hands of man.

Jesus is led before Pilate to glorify God. Even at the threat of death, He only spoke when and what the Father said to speak. He let it be known to Pilate and to whoever was around that there is no power but God, and that everything moves by the power of His Father. He went before Pilate in the meekness of the Spirit (power under control). He knew the Spirit was leading Him into suffering and death. He came into agreement with the fact that it was not a time to be exalted. Instead it was a time to glorify the Father.

In the New Covenant, God is glorified by the humiliation of flesh. We see this when Jesus would not defend Himself. To offer a defense in the power and authority of His Godhead would have defeated His very purpose for coming. Such a defense would have been birthed out of pride, in light of the fact that persecution, suffering and death were the very reasons for His coming.

As Jesus did, we too must learn to speak and do only those things that are edifying to purpose. To defend oneself against adversity relative to fulfilling your purpose is an act of vanity and an attempt at self-exaltation. To launch a wailing declaration, even with the truth, would be self-gratification and a sin against God.

Here is where we miss God so many times in the vanity of our words, speaking the truth in pride not love. Jesus not only had to be led by the Spirit but He also had to be governed by the Spirit. In order to fulfill righteousness He also had to walk by the Spirit. The Holy Ghost demanded that He only speak of the authority of God and not of Himself. In His heart Jesus sought to exalt the Father, therefore that decision was reflected in His response. Had Jesus exalted Himself by rehearsing the power that God had given Him He would have stepped outside the boundaries of the very Faith He came to establish.

WHY DOES GOD LEAD YOU INTO ADVERSITY?

I Peter 5:10

> *But the God of all grace, who hath called us unto his eternal glory by Christ Jesus, after that ye have suffered a while, make you perfect, stablish, strengthen, settle you.*

God will lead you into adversity (opposition) to establish you. We must understand that even with the Holy Ghost we must still be established in God. In the midst of adversity, this establishment is only by submission to the Father. You must understand that God will use situations to prove His power towards you. The suffering we endure has a purpose; often it is the trying of our faith. Your righteous response to the tests in your life will cause you to become settled and established in the Faith.

II Corinthians 1:3-7

> *3 Blessed be God, even the Father of our Lord Jesus Christ, the Father of mercies, and the God of all comfort;*
> *4 Who comforteth us in all our tribulation, that we may be able to comfort them which are in*

any trouble, by the comfort wherewith we ourselves are comforted of God.
5 For as the sufferings of Christ abound in us, so our consolation also aboundeth by Christ.
6 And whether we be afflicted, it is for your consolation and salvation, which is effectual in the enduring of the same sufferings which we also suffer: or whether we be comforted, it is for your consolation and salvation.
7 And our hope of you is stedfast, knowing, that as ye are partakers of the sufferings, so shall ye be also of the consolation.

Consider that this is another equally powerful reason for the Holy Ghost to lead you into affliction and sufferings for the gospel's sake. Paul states in the above passage that we are led into suffering for our brothers' consolation and salvation. Faith will console, save and comfort. When we endure and stand in faith it will have an effect on those who look upon us. Suffering in the flesh is a most effective way to preach the gospel.

Suffering in the flesh is to deny yourself the acts, emotions and responses of the flesh. When you are led by Faith you are comforted even inside tribulation. Faith will also allow you to comfort others who are in trouble. Would mere human trust and belief alone cause you to walk this way? No!!!! There are times when the faith of men fail. **The Faith of Christ will never fail.** It ministers beyond circumstances. The faith of Christ will bring peace in any situation and as others look at your life, they will find hope in the power of your faith.

As Sons of God we must realize that divine faith is our nature. We are not separated from the Faith of Christ in nature, character or emotion. Faith is who we are. Divine Faith is steadfast and unmovable; it will seek to glorify the Father by not allowing flesh to respond in situations and circumstances. This is a decision we must make, to walk by faith (the Spirit) or by sight (the way of flesh).

Psalm 119:67

> *Before I was afflicted I went astray: but now have I kept thy word.*

The chastening of the Lord is designed to kill the influence of flesh and cause the Sons to hide the Word in their hearts. As a result we will experience comfort through the power of the Word. This is how others will see God through us. Through our agreement with the Word in our hearts, we will manifest Christ in adversity. The world will see and have hope in God.

Psalm 119:165

> *Great peace have they which love thy law: and nothing shall offend them.*

Here is the conclusion to the matter. If you would just agree with God wholeheartedly, you would reveal the character of Christ in every adverse situation. You would not find yourself offended by any situation in which the Holy Spirit leads you, but rather you would find consolation in knowing that you are here to glorify the Father.

Chapter Twelve
APOSTOLIC ORDER

The Lord establishes the method by which deliverance is brought to His people. Many leaders in the Body of Christ have assumed this responsibility and have decided to devise their own method of deliverance. They have structured the Body as it has pleased them. The operation of the present Church is not the handiwork of God. It is the confusion and chaos of men.

THE LORD IS A GOD OF ORDER. This can be seen in the building of the tabernacle in the wilderness and in the establishing of the priesthood. The tribe of Levi numbered twenty-two thousand males. They were chosen to establish the first priesthood. The Lord instructed Moses how to separate their responsibilities. Each family of the Sons of Aaron was given specific tasks to perform in the tabernacle and the responsibility of each was different. Moses gave the assignments and it was he who knew the areas in which God wanted each member of the priesthood to work.

For this cause we have deacons and ministries of helps in the church today. Every man is chosen to serve according to his several God-given abilities. <u>These areas of responsibility were designed to bring order to the house</u>. It allowed all who were of the chosen tribe of Levi to work designated areas of ministry. **Each part worked together to perform the complete ministry to the people.**

As the Old Covenant is our schoolmaster, it is beneficial for us to note the principles illustrated here.

I. ESTABLISHING THE FIVE-FOLD MINISTRY

It is quite useful for us to go back to the Old Covenant to extract some of the <u>eternal principles</u> pertaining to ministry. To do this we will start with Jethro's advice to Moses concerning the people of God. At your leisure go back and read Exodus 18:13-26.

Now this account is relative to the fact that Moses was trying to counsel over six hundred thousand men and their families. Jethro's primary concern was for the physical well being of Moses and the people. He insisted that the task was too great for one man to handle. The same is true today. The task of leading and counseling the people of God is too much and too diversified for one person to handle.

However, I want us to note the <u>foundational counsel</u> he gave Moses:

1. Be thou for the people to Godward, that thou mayest bring their causes unto God:

➢ In other words, always point the people of God to their God.
➢ Allow the Lord to judge their causes or cases.

2. And thou shalt teach them ordinances and laws:

➢ Teach the people the Word of God. Keep it forever before them.

3. Shew them the way wherein they must walk:

➢ Teach them how to walk in the righteousness of God.

4. and the work that they must do:

➢ Show them the work they must do for the Lord.

These must be the attributes of the chief overseers of the people of God. They must have a mind to operate within the boundaries of the Word of God, never pointing the people to themselves. They must be willing to walk in the righteousness of God so that they will be living examples of that righteousness.

Jethro went on to instruct Moses as to how to choose those who would help in ministering to the people.

5. Moreover thou shalt provide out of all the people able men, such as fear God, men of truth, hating covetousness; and place such over them.

Notice the <u>character</u> of those who are to assist Moses.

1. **Able**: spiritually fit for service.
2. **Fear God**: they must have a fear of the Lord that will keep them from sinning against Him. This is the beginning of wisdom.
3. **Men of Truth**: they must love and respect the Word of God.
4. **Not covetous**: must want nothing, having no private agenda.

This must also be the character of those who purpose to serve in the Kingdom of God today.

II. INSTALLING THE GOVERNMENT

The Body of Christ is very similar to the nation of Israel as they came out of Egypt. We are the people of God, a holy nation unto God. Just as the Lord installed overseers over His people to teach them His laws and ways, the same is true today.

The Body of Christ is not without government. This government is a group of men and women chosen by God to teach the Body the mind and heart of the Father. They are instructed to contend for the faith of the common salvation that was ordained from the beginning of the world. Let us consider Ephesians 4:11-12 again. But this time we will read it from the Amplified version.

Ephesians 4:11-12
> *11 And His gifts were [varied; He Himself appointed and gave men to us] some to be apostles (special messengers), some prophets (inspired preachers and expounders), some evangelists (preachers of the Gospel, traveling missionaries), some pastors (shepherds of His flock) and teachers.*
> *12 His intention was the perfecting and the full equipping of the saints (His consecrated people), [that they should do] the work of ministering toward the building up Christ's body (the church),*

The above passages identify the ministries placed in the Body to oversee its development. It is the *apostles, prophets, evangelists, pastors* and *teachers* who are the governing body of the Church. These gifts represent the spiritual government installed by the Father to develop and govern His people. They are charged with bringing the Body to perfection or in other words, unto the measure of the stature of the fullness of Christ. **Sitting under these tutors should not leave us as children who are easily impressed by any doctrine or the cunning craftiness of men that are contrary to the truth.**

My brothers and sisters who carry the Word of God, I beseech you to allow this to be your reason for living. We should have no other agenda but to bring the people of God to perfection. We are not to become babysitters always feeding the flock with milk.

III. SETTING THE ORDER

Ephesians 4:5-11 identifies the government of God as the five-fold ministry gifts. However, the Lord takes this governmental body a little further in the book of I Corinthians.

I Corinthians 12:28
> *And God hath set some in the church, <u>first</u> apostles, <u>secondarily</u> prophets, <u>thirdly</u> (and <u>fourth</u>), teachers (pastors & teachers) after that), (<u>fifth</u>) miracles, then gifts of healings, (evangelists) helps, governments, diversities of tongues.*

In this passage the Lord reveals <u>the order in which the gifts are placed in the church</u>. First the *apostle*, which means that **the apostle's anointing is the foundational gift and head of the body government.** Now let us go back to Ephesians the 3rd chapter.

Ephesians 3:1-5

> *1 For this cause I Paul, the prisoner of Jesus Christ for you Gentiles,*
> *2 If ye have heard of the dispensation of the grace of God which is given me to youward:*
> *3 How that by revelation he made known unto me the mystery; (as I wrote afore in few words,*
> *4 Whereby, when ye read, ye may understand my knowledge in the mystery of Christ)*
> *5 Which in other ages was not made known unto the sons of men, as it is now revealed unto his holy apostles and prophets by the Spirit;*

Here Paul <u>confirms the order in which the revelation of the mystery of God was given to the church</u>. God revealed it first to His apostles and then, secondarily, to His prophets.

It is the *apostle* who wears the **foundational mantle** for the ministry. It is the *apostle* who installs, establishes and maintains the order in the church. This can be seen in all the writings of the New Testament epistles. Below is a brief summary of the purpose of the gifts to the Body.

➢ The **Apostle**: Establishes and maintains the order.
➢ The **Prophet**: Confirms the Word given to the church.
➢ The **Pastor**: Feeds the Word to the congregation.
➢ The **Teacher**: Further piece-meals the Word to the Body.
➢ The **Evangelist**: Compels men to come to Christ.

Of course, there is more to these gifts than the points stated above, but these are the most essential distinctions.

It is important that the principle of apostolic order be understood. I want you to visualize the human body. God has created the government in the Body of Christ in similar fashion to that of the human body. (See diagram on following page.)

CHRIST the **head**,
the APOSTLE as **the backbone**,
the PROPHET - **one arm**,
the PASTOR - **the other arm**,
the TEACHER - **one leg**
and the EVANGELIST - **the other leg.**

Please make note here that the head is attached to the backbone alone and that the rest of the limbs are attached to the backbone. This illustration symbolizes the fact that the revelation of Christ is given to the apostle first, confirmed by the prophet and fed to the rest of the Body by the pastors, teachers and evangelists.

Beloved, this is the order of God. It is His government. He will not exclude, overlook or disregard His order. The manna from heaven is going to come to His true apostles first and will be confirmed by His prophets. This is the method by which God chose to structure His government.

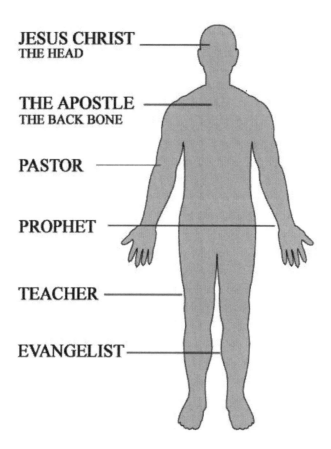

JESUS CHRIST
THE HEAD

THE APOSTLE
THE BACK BONE

PASTOR

PROPHET

TEACHER

EVANGELIST

APOSTOLIC ORDER
God's Government symbolized by the Human Skeleton

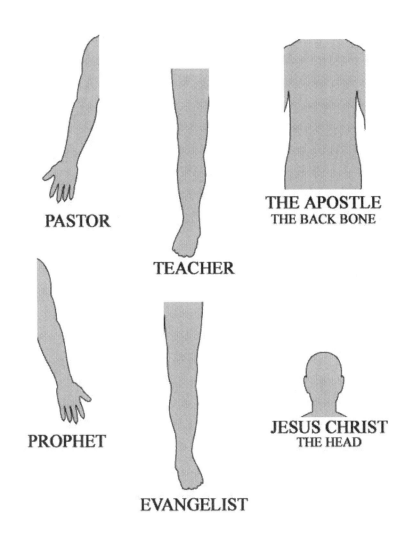

PASTOR

TEACHER

THE APOSTLE
THE BACK BONE

PROPHET

EVANGELIST

JESUS CHRIST
THE HEAD

The Church without Apostolic Order

DISJOINTED & DYSFUNCTIONAL

IV. A FRAGMENTED GOSPEL

Apostolic Order is God's method of governing His Body. However, this method is not being followed by the Body today, which explains why there are so many different belief systems in the Body of Christ. **When there is no apostolic order, pastors, teachers, evangelists and others can only rehash the same word over and over again.** They do not receive new and deeper revelation of the scriptures. Therefore, men are simply defining Hebrew and Greek words and calling that revelation.

The prophet is hearing his God and his own mind, for he has nothing to confirm or bear witness to. The apostles are running from church to church preaching but never establishing any order or government. They are never able to see an end result of the message, in the people they minister to. Thus, some have become frustrated with their own ministry.

When there is no established apostolic order another misfortune seems to overtake the apostle, the prophet, the pastors, evangelists and teachers. There seems to be a pattern of spiritualizing that carries whatever they have heard in the spirit to another dimension which borders on, and in some cases crosses the line of heresy.

It is important for every minister of the gospel to know that this is the order of God and He will not deviate from it. **THE TRUE REVELATION OF JESUS CHRIST IS GOING TO COME THROUGH THIS ORDER ONLY.** Anything else is simply a fragmentation of the gospel.

A fragmented gospel can get sinners saved but will not enable them to endure to the end. The fragmentation of the five-fold ministry has caused the Body of Christ to fail in its purpose to glorify the Father. The world is not sure of the Church being the manifold wisdom of God. It has seen division, wars, sin and iniquity that equals its own.

V. ALL SPEAKING THE SAME THING

It is the government of God in the Body that is to bring order and unity. Apostolic order guarantees that all will speak the same thing and come into a singleness of heart, mind and purpose.

The early church all spoke the same things. The gospel was not fragmented. The apostles set the order and delivered the revelation of the mystery of God. They produced power in the people they ministered to. Many of the early Christians had power to become martyrs for the sake of the gospel. They denied themselves of the things of this life and submitted to a life of suffering and degradation as necessary, but moreover they demonstrated the power to live holy.

Pastors, I challenge you to take a good look at what you preach and what it is producing. Are you really receiving fresh manna from heaven or are you teaching the same messages that have been taught for years with an added twist or flare? Have you been able to teach God's people how to live and walk in His Spirit on a daily basis?

Be honest with yourself. Are you experiencing what seems to be a void in your knowledge and your service to God? Have you noticed that there is something missing, but you cannot seem to point it out? You find yourself desiring more, but what "it" actually is seems to evade you. There may be a word inside of you that you cannot seem to articulate. You may even teach bits and pieces of revelations that you have never heard anyone mention. Believe it or not, this is good. The Holy Ghost has created a hunger and thirst in you for the deeper things of God. **If your motive for wanting to know the deeper truths is pure, God will lead you to the fountain that flows continuously with the manna from on high.** He will lead you to sit under the mantle of a real apostle. He will lead you to apostolic order.

Chapter Thirteen
THE LAST REFORMATION

It is imperative that you begin to consider that you are in the midst of a reformation. In fact, you have been called to be a reformer. It is the Word of God that you will minister to the Body and the world that will turn the hearts of men to the Father. Our time is even as that of John the Baptist. We are the messengers sent to tell the good news of salvation and life through the coming Savior. He is soon to return to claim His own but you cannot deliver such a message without becoming the evidence of that life. You must cease to walk in that old mindset which causes you to vacillate in and out of the righteousness of God.

The mindset of the Sons of God in this day must be that of reformation. It is time for the true Sons to take responsibility for the disposition of the Body of Christ. We are the called of God and have been given much by the Father. We must take heed to the signs of the times, for the end is near. This age is rapidly coming to an end. Jesus, having anticipated these times asked, ***"Nevertheless when the Son of man cometh, shall he find faith on the earth?" (St. Luke 18:8)***. Will there be those who are walking in the mind of Christ?

GLOBALIZATION

The Sons must think in terms of getting the truth to every nation on earth. We have been given the revelation of Christ and have taken on His mind. It is our responsibility to carry His mind to the Church first, and then the world. The Church, itself, has been led off course with divers doctrines of men and has become self-serving, without regard for the eternal purpose of God. *Go ye into all the world, and preach the gospel to every creature (St. Mark 16:15).* This is the commission we have today.

The technology is in place and the comprehension of the message is real. All that is left is to obey. We, the truly manifested Sons of God must not forfeit our opportunity to glorify the Father. We must not be as those who talk a good game, but deliver nothing. Opportunities are being offered to us to utilize every bit of our influence, substance, resources and strengths to get this message to the masses. The Body of Christ will turn back to the heart of the Father. It will come to the unity of the faith and it will become blameless and perfected in love. The Father will have Himself a people who will obey and there are many of us who are committed to working God's vision on the earth.

REFORM AND RENEWAL

The reformation of the Church begins with the reformed life of each of its members. The following text is what I consider to be the heart of the reformation message as it focuses on the life and mindset of the Sons of God.

Ephesians 4:11-13
> *11 And he gave some, apostles; and some, prophets; and some, evangelists; and some, pastors and teachers;*
> *12 For the perfecting of the saints, for the work of the ministry, for the edifying of the body of Christ:*
> *13 Till we all come in the unity of the faith, and of the knowledge of the Son of God, unto a*

perfect man, unto the measure of the stature of the fulness of Christ:

How many more lessons, sermons, counseling sessions or conferences will it take to get you to embrace the knowledge of the Son of God that you have already received? At some point you must accept that there are others in the Body of Christ who are walking in the unity of the faith and presenting to the Father a perfected life. Just because you may not have accepted it as purpose for your life, does not mean that the reformation of the Body is on hold. The Lord is going to have Himself a people. In fact, He does have a people who are living holy everyday. They have come to believe what the Word of God says about them and in doing so have taken on the mind of Christ.

These Sons have probably not been made known to the Body or the world as yet, but you can believe that they soon will be. The time has for them to be exposed to the Church and the world. The Lord is now shooting them out of His quiver as fiery arrows into the darkness of this world.

Ephesians 4:14
> *That we henceforth be no more children, tossed to and fro, and carried about with every wind of doctrine, by the sleight of men, and cunning craftiness, whereby they lie in wait to deceive;*

How is it possible for you who are so knowledgeable of the Word, to be deceived by the doctrines and cunning craftiness of men? It is time to face the truth. To be deceived regarding your walk in the Word is to lessen the evil that is in the sin you commit or the want that is in your heart. It is evil when there is something that stands between you and doing the will of the Father. You must cease to justify mindsets and dispositions that are clearly not the mind of Christ. Your own actions and emotions are the signs that you are not walking in the Spirit. The reality is that you have preferred to walk after the flesh.

There is no way around the fact that walking in the Spirit is the dissolution of divers mindsets and the craftiness of men. Christ always walked in the wisdom of God. When you walk in the Spirit, you too, will walk in the same wisdom. The want for the things of this world will no longer exist and the love of God for His people will manifest without reservation.

Ephesians 4:15

> *But speaking the truth in love, may grow up into him in all things, which is the head, even Christ:*

Those who are called to lead must live the truth they speak. The manifestation of this is a walk of love. There is no learning Christ without walking in the love of Christ, which is within you. To reject the walk in the Spirit is to never achieve righteousness or purpose.

Ephesians 4:16-17

> *16 From whom the whole body fitly joined together and compacted by that which every joint supplieth, according to the effectual working in the measure of every part, maketh increase of the body unto the edifying of itself in love.*

17 This I say therefore, and testify in the Lord, that ye henceforth walk not as other Gentiles walk, in the vanity of their mind,

The New Creature was subjected to, or forced to remain in this fleshy body. This body has a mind and memory of the sins and pleasures it has experienced, but the New Man is created in Christ Jesus. The Word instructs us to put on the mind of Christ. Where do we put it on? When we walk in the Spirit the mind of Christ controls the flesh. Its power is greater than that of the fleshy mind and it is able to subdue all unlawful desires engendered in the flesh by wrong thinking. The mind of Christ experiences no controversy regarding obedience to the Father and His Word.

To walk in the vanity of your natural mind (carnal mind) is to remain void of the life and love of Christ. You will not be able to manifest the love for mankind that is necessary to minister effectively to the Church or the world.

Ephesians 4:18
Having the understanding darkened, being alienated from the life of God through the ignorance that is in them, because of the blindness of their heart:

To treasure what you want, think, or feel will alienate you from the life of God. If you hold your desires, feelings and thoughts so dear, you will simply refuse to relinquish them in exchange for the mind of Christ. It is amazing how you convince yourself of a sense of loss when these are to be forsaken. Remember, the carnal mind is enmity against God. Only the Spirit of God is able to subdue the mind of the flesh and bring it into submission to the will and way of God.

When you walk in the Spirit, the New Man is manifested. Otherwise, you will always be at war with the temptations of the flesh. If you have been trained in the truth, the fleshy mind has comprehended that training as well. It knows the Word but is often not able to resist temptation without the power of the Spirit. This is also where much deception appears. Many think that because they have made some right decisions concerning sin and lust, it is all right to operate within the confines of the fleshy mind. The fleshy mind is vulnerable to the desires of the members of flesh therefore it is imperative that it be exposed to the Holy Spirit for power and consistency.

Ephesians 4:19

> *Who being past feeling have given themselves over unto lasciviousness, to work all uncleanness with greediness.*

Again, this is what happens when you try to operate without walking in the Spirit. Eventually there will be a giving over to that area of vulnerability. When this happens, don't think the fleshy mind is going to war against itself with any degree of success. Instead, it will devise a plan that puts it in hot pursuit of the things it wants to accomplish.

All of this drama and spiritual trauma can be avoided by simply maintaining your walk in the Spirit. By doing so, you are not vulnerable to mindsets or temptations that destroy your relationship with the Father. Christ has already overcome the world and you are an overcomer if you walk in Him.

Ephesians 4:20-24

> *20 But ye have not so learned Christ;*

21 If so be that ye have heard him, and have been taught by him, as the truth is in Jesus:
22 That ye put off concerning the former conversation the old man, which is corrupt according to the deceitful lusts;
23 And be renewed in the spirit of your mind;
24 And that ye put on the new man, which after God is created in righteousness and true holiness.

It is the responsibility of the New Man to allow the mind of Christ to control the flesh. This is the choice you have to make. I can promise you that in doing so you will not experience a sense of loss. You will know contentment and the joy of obedience to the Word. The love of God will flow from you without stress or restraint. You will be happy walking in a power that can and will adequately resist temptation. Beloved, take hold of these truths, walk before our God and BE YE PERFECT.

Made in the USA
Columbia, SC
12 January 2023

10162021R00076